CONTENTS

Cheese
please

Cheese
please

the ultimate cheese lover's recipe collection

ROZ DENNY

southwater

This edition is published by Southwater

Distributed in the UK by
The Manning Partnership
251–253 London Road East
Batheaston
Bath BA1 7RL
tel. 01225 852 727
fax 01225 852 852

Published in the USA by
Anness Publishing Inc.
27 West 20th Street
Suite 504
New York
NY 10011
fax 212 807 6813

Distributed in Canada by
General Publishing
895 Don Mills Road
400–402 Park Centre
Toronto, Ontario M3C 1W3
tel. 416 445 3333
fax 416 445 5991

Distributed in Australia by
Sandstone Publishing
Unit 1, 360 Norton Street
Leichhardt
New South Wales 2040
tel. 02 9560 7888
fax 02 9560 7488

Southwater is an imprint of Anness Publishing Limited
Hermes House, 88–89 Blackfriars Road, London SE1 8HA
tel. 020 7401 2077; fax 020 7633 9499

© Anness Publishing Limited 2001

PUBLISHER Joanna Lorenz
MANAGING EDITOR Judith Simons
PROJECT EDITOR Mariano Kälfors
DESIGNER Nigel Partridge
PHOTOGRAPHY John Heseltine and William Lingwood
HOME ECONOMIST Carole Handslip
JACKET DESIGNER The Bridgewater Book Company Limited
PRODUCTION CONTROLLER Claire Rae
EDITORIAL READER Joy Wotton

Previously published as part of a larger compendium,
The World Encyclopedia of Cheese

10 9 8 7 6 5 4 3 2 1

- Bracketed terms are intended for American readers
- For all recipes, quantities are given in both metric and imperial
  measures, and, where appropriate, measures are also given in standard
  cups and spoons. Follow one set, but not a mixture, because they are
  not interchangeable.
- Standard spoon and cup measurements are level.
  1 tsp = 5ml, 1 tbsp = 15ml, 1 cup = 250ml/8fl oz
- Australian standard tablespoons are 20ml. Australian readers should
  use 3 tsp in place of 1 tbsp for measuring small quantities of gelatine,
  flour, salt etc.
- Medium (US large) eggs are used unless otherwise stated.

INTRODUCTION

In shops and markets around the world, thousands of cheeses tempt our eyes and challenge our tastebuds. Wrinkled and mouldy, smooth and sunshine yellow, orange and smelly or brilliant white, they are all labelled cheese, and their shapes and sizes, flavours and textures range from the sublime to the truly extraordinary.

Cheese is such a wonderful ingredient that there is little to beat it as a food on its own, and most cheeses are best eaten simply with bread or fruit. However, there are some excellent cooking cheeses. A few, especially some fresh cheeses, are even better cooked than uncooked as their taste and texture act as a foil for other ingredients to shine. The recipes that follow are by no means meant to be exhaustive: to record every cheese and their culinary use around the world would be an impossible, if pleasurable, task. Many of the dishes featured are quick and simple, but also included are some wonderful, classic dishes that have stood the test of time, as well other more up-tempo dishes, which are appropriate for modern life-styles.

SOUPS
AND SNACKS

Place cheese between slices of fresh bread for sandwiches, crumble it on top of soup, stuff cubes of it into hot baked potatoes, and you have some idea of how you can use a wonderful food quickly and elegantly. These recipes are great for many simple meals such as brunches and suppers, picnics and even easy entertaining.

25g/1oz/2 tbsp butter
1 onion, chopped
1 potato, peeled and chopped
500g/1¼lb/2 heads of broccoli,
or purple sprouting
broccoli, chopped
1 litre/1¾ pints/4 cups water
100g/3¾oz Maytag Blue cheese,
rind removed, and cubed
freshly grated nutmeg
salt and ground black pepper
a little walnut oil, to serve

SERVES 4

VARIATION
Use Stilton or a milder blue cheese
such as Dolcelatte or Bleu d'Causses.

50g/2oz/¼ cup butter
2 onions, about 250g/9oz, sliced
10ml/2 tsp plain (all-purpose) flour
1 litre/1¾ pints/4 cups vegetable or
chicken stock
60ml/4 tbsp dry white wine or
30ml/2 tbsp dry sherry
4 slices crusty white bread
150g/5oz Gruyère or Emmental
cheese, grated
salt and ground black pepper

SERVES 4

COOK'S TIPS
To give the soup a good colour, make
sure the onions are lightly browned
before you add the stock.
Cheddar could be substituted for
Gruyère or Emmental, but the
soup would no longer be
strictly authentic.

BROCCOLI AND MAYTAG BLUE SOUP

Broccoli is such a flavoursome vegetable that it needs little by way of additional ingredients to make a tasty soup. However, the creamy tang of a blue cheese makes it quite special.

1 Heat the butter in a large pan and stir in the onion and potato. Cover and cook gently for 5 minutes, then add the broccoli and cook for another 5 minutes. Add the water, bring to the boil, season and simmer for 15 minutes.

2 Strain, reserving the liquid. Put the cooked vegetables in a food processor and moisten with a little of the cooking liquid. Process until very silky and smooth. With the motor running, gradually add the remaining cooking liquid through the feeder tube.

3 Strain the soup back into the clean pan. Reheat until nearly boiling, then remove from the heat.

4 Stir in the cheese until melted. Add nutmeg, salt and pepper to taste. Serve in four warmed bowls with a trickle of walnut oil in each.

FRENCH ONION SOUP

Bread and cheese soups are popular in many countries. One of the great classics is the soup made famous in Les Halles in Paris. It is sold there today, although sadly the market itself has moved on. It is always served with a lightly chewy topping of melted Gruyère.

1 Melt the butter in a large pan. Add the onions and cook for about 12 minutes or until lightly browned. Stir in the flour and continue to cook until the flour turns a sandy colour.

2 Pour in the stock and wine or sherry and bring to the boil, stirring. Season, cover and simmer for 15 minutes.

3 Preheat the grill (broiler). Lightly toast the bread. Divide the cheese among them. Return to the grill and heat until the cheese is bubbling. Place in four warmed, heatproof bowls.

4 Remove the onions from the soup and divide them among the bowls. Pour the soup and serve immediately.

2 thick slices of bread
a little unsalted (sweet) butter,
for spreading
100g/3¾oz Cheddar, sliced
10ml/2 tsp spicy or mild mustard or
good pinch of paprika or
cayenne pepper
ground black pepper

SERVES 2

*Cheddar is an excellent cheese
for melting.*

130g/4½oz Cheddar or similar
cheese, grated
10ml/2 tsp plain (all-purpose) flour
10ml/2 tsp mild mustard
60ml/4 tbsp beer or milk
4 thick slices of country-
style bread
good pinch of paprika or
cayenne pepper
fresh basil leaves and tomato
wedges, to garnish

SERVES 4

VARIATIONS
For Buck Rarebit, top Traditional
Welsh Rarebit with a poached egg and
perhaps a rasher (strip) or two of
bacon. For a more upbeat presentation,
top plain Welsh Rarebit with roasted
(bell) peppers or plum tomatoes, or
caramelized red onions. Serve with a
mixed herb and green leaf salad.

WELSH RAREBIT

Also called Welsh Rabbit, this is a popular British snack and is made in a wide variety of ways. Use a good melting cheese, such as Cheddar, Lancashire, Monterey Jack, Cheshire or Caerphilly.

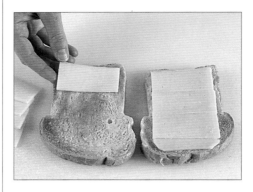

1 Preheat the grill (broiler) and lightly toast the bread on both sides. Spread sparingly with butter, then top with the cheese, leaving a narrow border around the edges. Heat under the grill until the cheese melts and starts to brown.

2 Spread the cheese quickly with some mustard or sprinkle with a little paprika or cayenne. Add a grinding of pepper. Cut in half diagonally and serve immediately.

TRADITIONAL WELSH RAREBIT

Toasted bread can also be topped with a deliciously rich, creamy cheese sauce, which can be made with either beer or milk. Beer gives the sauce a mellow, hoppy taste and a wonderful country flavour.

1 Preheat the grill (broiler). Mix the cheese, flour and mustard in a small pan. Pour in the beer or milk and stir well.

2 Heat gently, stirring until thick and creamy. Do not allow it to boil. Toast the bread lightly under the grill. Pour the melted cheese on to the toast and spread to the edges. Return to the grill and cook until the cheese is browned.

3 Sprinkle the grilled cheese with paprika or cayenne and serve at once, garnished with basil and tomatoes.

CROQUE MONSIEUR

A popular French snack that literally translated means "crunch (or munch) gentleman". This is an easy dish for children to prepare, especially when a sandwich toaster is used.

1 Preheat a sandwich toaster or the grill (broiler). Lightly butter the bread and lay the cheese and ham on two of the slices. Top with the other slices of bread and press firmly together.

2 Cook in the sandwich toaster, following the manufacturer's instructions, or grill until browned on both sides. Serve hot, garnished with parsley.

a little butter, for spreading
4 thin slices of country-style bread
75g/3oz Gruyère or Cheddar cheese, sliced
2 lean honey roast ham slices
ground black pepper
flat leaf parsley, to garnish

SERVES 2

BELOW: Traditional Welsh Rarebit (LEFT) and Croque Monsieur (RIGHT).

MEXICAN TACOS

Ready-made taco shells make perfect edible containers for shredded salad, meat fillings, grated cheese and sour cream. For an authentic touch, use Mexican queso blanco or queso anejado.

15ml/1 tbsp olive oil
250g/9oz lean minced (ground) beef or turkey
2 garlic cloves, crushed
5ml/1 tsp ground cumin
5–10ml/1–2 tsp mild chilli powder
8 ready-made taco shells
1/2 small iceberg lettuce, shredded
1 small onion, thinly sliced
2 tomatoes, chopped in chunks
1 avocado, halved, stoned (pitted) and sliced
60ml/4 tbsp/ 1/4 cup sour cream
125g/4oz/1 cup crumbled queso blanco or anejado, or grated Cheddar or Monterey Jack cheese
salt and ground black pepper
SERVES 4

1 Heat the oil in a frying pan. Add the meat, with the garlic and spices, and brown over a medium heat, stirring frequently to break up any lumps. Season, cook for 5 minutes, then set aside to cool slightly.

2 Meanwhile, warm the taco shells according to the instructions on the packet. Do not let them get too crisp. Spoon the lettuce, onion, tomatoes and avocado slices into the taco shells. Top with the sour cream followed by the minced beef or turkey mixture.

3 Sprinkle the crumbled or grated cheese into the tacos and serve immediately. Tacos are eaten with the fingers, so have plenty of paper napkins handy.

FONTINA PAN BAGNA

When the weather is hot, a crusty flute or baguette filled with juicy tomatoes, crisp red onion, green pepper, thinly sliced Fontina and sliced black olives makes a refreshing snack.

1 small red onion, thinly sliced
1 fresh flute or baguette
extra virgin olive oil
3 ripe plum tomatoes, thinly sliced
1 small green (bell) pepper, cored, halved and thinly sliced
200g/7oz Fontina cheese, thinly sliced
about 12 pitted black olives, sliced
a handful of flat leaf parsley or basil leaves
salt and ground black pepper

SERVES 2–4

VARIATIONS
Instead of Fontina, try Havarti, or Taleggio. Use chopped canned anchovies instead of olives.

1 Soak the red onion in plenty of cold water for at least an hour, then drain well in a colander, tip on to kitchen paper and pat dry.

2 Slice the flute or baguette in half lengthways and brush the cut sides well with olive oil. Lay the tomato slices down one side and season well.

3 Top with the pepper slices followed by the onion slices, then add the cheese and olives. Scatter over the parsley or basil leaves and season again.

4 Press the halves together, then wrap tightly in clear film (plastic wrap) to compress. Chill for 1 hour. Unwrap and cut diagonally in thick slices to serve.

MOZZARELLA IN CAROZZA WITH FRESH TOMATO SALSA

200g/7oz mozzarella cheese,
thinly sliced
8 thin slices of bread,
crusts removed
a little dried oregano
30ml/2 tbsp freshly grated
Parmesan cheese
3 eggs, beaten
olive oil, for frying
salt and ground black pepper
fresh herbs, to garnish

FOR THE SALSA
4 ripe plum tomatoes, peeled, seeded
and finely chopped
15ml/1 tbsp chopped fresh parsley
5ml/1 tsp balsamic vinegar
15ml/1 tbsp extra virgin olive oil

SERVES 4

The title of this delectable Italian snack translates as cheese "in a carriage". The recipe is similar to Croque Monsieur except that it contains mozzarella and is dipped in beaten egg and fried like French toast.

1 Arrange the mozzarella on four slices of the bread. Season with salt and pepper and sprinkle with a little dried oregano and the Parmesan. Top with the other bread slices and press them firmly together.

2 Pour the beaten eggs into a large shallow dish and season with salt and pepper. Add the cheese sandwiches, two at a time, pressing them into the egg with a fish slice (spatula) until they are well coated. Repeat with the remaining sandwiches, then leave them to stand for 10 minutes.

3 To make the salsa, put the chopped tomatoes in a bowl and add the parsley. Stir in the vinegar and the extra virgin olive oil. Season well with salt and pepper and set aside.

4 Heat olive oil to a depth of 5mm/¼in in a large frying pan. Carefully add the sandwiches in batches and cook for about 2 minutes on each side until golden and crisp. Drain well on kitchen paper. Cut in half and serve garnished with fresh herbs and accompanied by the salsa.

CHEESE AIGRETTES

These choux buns, flavoured with mature Gruyère and dusted with grated Parmesan, are a bit fiddly to make, but the dough can be prepared ahead and then deep fried to serve. They make a wonderful party snack.

100g/3¾oz/scant 1 cup strong white bread flour
2.5ml/½ tsp paprika
2.5ml/½ tsp salt
75g/3oz/6 tbsp cold butter, diced
200ml/7fl oz/scant 1 cup water
3 eggs, beaten
75g/3oz/¾ cup coarsely grated mature (aged) Gruyère cheese
corn or vegetable oil, for deep frying
50g/2oz piece of Parmesan cheese, finely grated
ground black pepper
sprigs of flat leaf parsley, to garnish

MAKES 30

VARIATION
Make slightly larger aigrettes, slit them open and scoop out any soft paste. Fill the centres with taramasalata or crumbled Roquefort mixed with a little fromage frais or cream cheese.

1 Sift the flour, paprika and salt on to a sheet of baking parchment. Add a generous grinding of pepper.

2 Put the butter and water into a medium pan and heat gently. As soon as the butter has melted and the liquid starts to boil, add the seasoned flour at once and beat hard with a wooden spoon until the dough comes away from the sides of the pan.

3 Remove the pan from the heat and cool the paste for 5 minutes. This step is important if the aigrettes are to rise well. Gradually beat in enough of the beaten egg to give a stiff dropping consistency that still holds a shape on the spoon. Mix in the Gruyère.

4 Heat the oil for deep frying to 180°C/350°F. Take a teaspoonful of the choux paste and use a second spoon to slide it into the oil. Make more aigrettes in the same way. Fry for 3–4 minutes until golden brown. Drain on kitchen paper and keep warm while cooking successive batches. To serve, pile the aigrettes on a warmed serving dish, sprinkle with Parmesan and garnish with sprigs of parsley.

2 red onions, sliced
5ml/1 tsp sugar
90ml/6 tbsp red wine vinegar
2.5ml/1/2 tsp salt
generous pinch of dried dill
500g/11/4lb new potatoes, halved if
large, scrubbed
250g/9oz raclette cheese slices
salt and ground black pepper
selection of salamis, garlic
sausages or country-style ham,
to serve

SERVES 4

COOK'S TIP
Look for ready-sliced raclette for
this dish – it is available from most
large supermarkets and specialist
cheese shops.

200g/7oz can tuna, drained
and flaked
1 spring onion (scallion), chopped
1 small celery stick, chopped
15ml/1 tbsp chopped canned
pimiento or 1 medium
tomato, chopped
30ml/2 tbsp mayonnaise
generous pinch of dried oregano
or marjoram
2 wholemeal (whole-wheat)
muffins, split
65g/21/2oz mature Monterey Jack or
Cheddar cheese, coarsely grated
or sliced
8 pimiento- or anchovy-stuffed
olives, sliced
salt and ground black pepper

SERVES 2

RACLETTE WITH NEW POTATOES

*Made in both Switzerland and France, raclette melts to a velvety creaminess
and warm golden colour. Melted over hot new potatoes and served with cold
meats and red onion pickle, it makes the ideal quick meal.*

1 First, make the pickle. Spread out
the onions in a dish, pour over boiling
water to cover and leave to soak until
cold. Meanwhile, mix the sugar, vinegar,
salt and dill in a small pan. Heat gently,
stirring until the sugar has dissolved,
then cool. Drain the onions, pour the
vinegar mixture over, cover and leave
for at least 1 hour, preferably overnight.

2 Boil the potatoes in their skins, then
drain and place in a roasting tin.
Preheat the grill (broiler). Season the
potatoes and arrange the raclette on
top. Place under the heat until the
cheese melts. Serve hot with sliced
cold meats. Drain the excess vinegar
from the pickled red onion and serve
the pickle with the potatoes.

TUNA MELT MUFFINS

*Try this delicious and nutritious snack consisting of wholemeal muffins
topped with tuna and hot bubbling cheese. Use wholemeal (whole-wheat) toast
in place of the muffins, if you like.*

1 Mix the tuna with the spring onion,
celery, pimiento or tomato, mayonnaise
and oregano or marjoram. Stir in salt
and pepper to taste, then set aside.

2 Preheat the grill (broiler) and toast
the cut side of the muffins until golden.

3 Spoon a quarter of the tuna mixture
on to each muffin half, then top with
the cheese and stuffed olive slices. Grill
until the cheese has melted and is
bubbling. There is no need to brown
the cheese. Serve hot, sprinkled with
more black pepper.

SALADS AND
VEGETABLE DISHES

Cheese has an affinity with vegetables. Many cheeses taste best uncooked and at room temperature, so they are ideal for using in salads and look sensational tossed into crisp green leaves and colourful salad vegetables. However, cheeses can also be turned into satisfying hot main dishes, stirred into simple sauces and used to coat lightly cooked vegetables.

CAESAR SALAD

Not a classic dish of ancient Roman times, but a salad created in America in the 1920s by a restaurateur called Caesar Cardini. Fresh Parmesan is an essential ingredient, as is cold cos or Romaine lettuce.

2 large garlic cloves, halved
45ml/3 tbsp extra virgin olive oil
4 slices of wholemeal
(whole-wheat) bread
1 small cos or 2 Romaine lettuces
50g/2oz piece of Parmesan cheese,
shaved or coarsely grated

FOR THE DRESSING
1 egg
10ml/2 tsp Dijon mustard
5ml/1 tsp Worcestershire sauce
30ml/2 tbsp fresh lemon juice
30ml/2 tbsp extra virgin olive oil
salt and ground black pepper

SERVES 4

VARIATIONS
Anchovies could be added to the salad. Drain a 50g/2oz can and cut the anchovies into long, thin strips. Pat dry using kitchen paper. Instead of adding a semi-raw egg to the dressing, hard-boil 2 eggs, peel and quarter them and use in the salad itself.

1 Preheat the oven to 190°C/375°F/Gas 5. Rub the inside of a salad bowl with one of the half cloves of garlic. Mix the oil with the remaining garlic in a small pan and heat for 5 minutes, then remove the garlic.

2 Remove the crusts from the bread and cut the slices into small cubes. Toss these in the garlic-flavoured oil, making sure that they are well coated. Spread out the bread cubes on a baking sheet, bake for about 10 minutes until crisp, then leave to cool.

3 Separate the lettuces leaves, wash and dry them and arrange in a shallow salad bowl.

4 To make the dressing, boil the egg for 1 minute only. Crack it into a bowl, using a teaspoon to scoop out any softly set white. Using a balloon whisk, beat in the mustard, Worcestershire sauce, lemon juice, olive oil and salt and pepper. Sprinkle the Parmesan over the salad and drizzle the dressing over. Scatter with the croûtons. Take the salad to the table, toss lightly and serve immediately.

TRICOLOUR SALAD

A popular salad, this dish depends for its success on the quality of its ingredients. Mozzarella di bufala is the best cheese to serve uncooked. Whole ripe plum tomatoes give up their juice to blend with extra virgin olive oil for a natural dressing.

150g/5oz mozzarella di bufala cheese, thinly sliced
4 large plum tomatoes, sliced
sea salt flakes, to season
1 large avocado
about 12 basil leaves
or a small handful of flat leaf parsley leaves
45–60ml/3–4 tbsp extra virgin olive oil
ground black pepper

SERVES 2

1 Arrange the sliced cheese and tomatoes randomly on two salad plates. Crush over a few good pinches of sea salt flakes. This will help to draw out some of the juices from the tomatoes. Set aside in a cool place to marinate for about 30 minutes.

2 Just before serving, cut the avocado in half using a large sharp knife and twist to separate. Lift out the stone (pit) and remove the peel.

3 Slice the avocado flesh crossways into half moons, or cut it into large chunks if that is easier.

4 Place the avocado on the salad, then sprinkle with the basil or parsley. Drizzle over the olive oil, add a little more salt if liked and some black pepper. Serve at room temperature, with chunks of crusty Italian ciabatta.

VARIATIONS
A light sprinkling of balsamic vinegar added just before serving gives the salad a refreshing tang, while a few thinly sliced red onion rings would add extra colour and flavour.

ROQUEFORT AND BEAN SALAD WITH HONEY DRESSING

Pungent and creamy, classic sheep's milk Roquefort from the Massif Centrale of France makes an excellent salad cheese. It goes particularly well with pale green flageolet beans and a light sweet-sour dressing.

150g/5oz/scant 1 cup dried flageolet (small cannellini) beans, soaked overnight in water to cover
1 bay leaf
1 sprig of thyme
1 small onion, sliced
30ml/2 tbsp chopped fresh parsley
30ml/2 tbsp chopped walnuts
200g/7oz Roquefort cheese, lightly crumbled
salt and ground black pepper
red and green salad leaves, to serve

FOR THE DRESSING
60ml/4 tbsp extra virgin olive oil
30ml/2 tbsp rice wine vinegar or half wine vinegar and half water
5ml/1 tsp Dijon mustard
10ml/2 tsp clear honey

SERVES 4

1 Drain the beans and place in a pan. Pour in cold water to cover. Bring to the boil. Cook over a medium heat for 10 minutes, then reduce the heat. Add the bay leaf, thyme and onion and simmer for 20–25 minutes, 45 if using small cannellini beans, or until tender.

2 Drain the beans, discarding the herbs but not the onion. Tip into a bowl, season and leave until just warm.

3 Make the dressing. Mix the oil, vinegar or vinegar and water, mustard and honey in a small bowl. Add salt to taste and a generous grinding of pepper. Pour over the beans. Add the parsley and walnuts.

4 Gently mix the crumbled Roquefort into the salad. Serve the salad at room temperature accompanied by red and green salad leaves.

VARIATIONS
Any other sheep's milk blue cheese could be used instead of Roquefort. The salad is also delicious with either cooked green or Puy lentils instead of the beans.

TOASTED CROTTINS WITH BEETROOT SALAD

Crottins grill to a delicious, nutty creaminess in a matter of minutes for serving on thinly sliced walnut bread toast. A salad of grated raw beetroot makes a colourful accompaniment.

raw beetroots (beets), about 200g/7oz
1 celery stick
2 spring onions (scallions)
60ml/4 tbsp French dressing
generous pinch of ground cumin
4 small slices of walnut bread
a little butter, for spreading
4 crottins (small goat's milk cheeses), about 60g/2¼oz each
salt and ground black pepper
rocket (arugula) or watercress leaves, to serve

SERVES 4

1 Peel the beetroots and grate coarsely. Ideally, the beetroot should be served raw, but, if you prefer, blanch it in boiling water for 3 minutes, then drain, refresh under cold running water and drain again. Put the beetroot in a bowl.

2 Slice the celery and spring onions finely and toss with the beetroot, dressing and cumin. Add salt and pepper to taste. Leave to marinate for an hour or so, if possible, then mound on to four salad plates.

3 Preheat the grill (broiler). Toast the walnut bread lightly on each side. Keep warm. Place a sheet of foil on the rack, add the crottins and grill for 3–5 minutes until they turn golden brown on top and just start to melt.

4 Meanwhile, butter the toast lightly. Place on the plates, then, using a palette knife (spatula), transfer the crottins to the toast and serve immediately with the beetroot salad and the rocket or watercress leaves.

HOT HALLOUMI WITH ROASTED PEPPERS

selection of 6 (bell) peppers, red, green or yellow
olive oil
30ml/2 tbsp balsamic or red wine vinegar
small handful of raisins (optional)
300g/11oz Halloumi cheese, thickly sliced
salt and ground black pepper
flat leaf parsley, to garnish
sesame seed bread, to serve (optional)

SERVES 4

COOK'S TIPS

For a crisp coating on the Halloumi, toss the slices in plain (all-purpose) flour before frying them. Plain Halloumi can be grilled instead of fried. Simply preheat a grill or ridged grilling pan, add the cheese slices and cook until golden brown, turning once. They are also good barbecued.

The best-known cheese from Cyprus is the salty, hard Halloumi. Delicious served simply sliced or cubed, it takes on a wonderful texture when grilled (broiled) or fried. Roasted sweet peppers makes a fine accompaniment.

1 Preheat the oven to 220°C/425°F/ Gas 7. Cut the peppers in quarters, discard the cores and seeds, then place cut side down on a non-stick baking sheet. Roast for 15–20 minutes until the skins start to blacken and blister. Remove and cover with several layers of kitchen paper. Set aside for 30 minutes, then peel off the skins. Slice the flesh into a bowl. Save any roasting juices and mix these with the peppers.

2 Pour a little olive oil over the peppers. Add the vinegar and raisins, if used, with salt and pepper to taste. Toss lightly and leave to cool.

3 When ready to serve, divide the pepper salad among four plates. Heat olive oil to a depth of about 5mm/¼in in a large heavy-based frying pan. Fry the Halloumi slices over a medium-high heat for about 2–3 minutes, turning them halfway through cooking until golden brown on both sides.

4 Drain the Halloumi thoroughly on kitchen paper and serve with the roasted peppers and a parsley garnish. Accompany with chunks of sesame seed bread, if desired.

LENTIL, TOMATO AND CHEESE SALAD

Lentils and cheese are a natural combination. The small blue-green Puy lentils from France are perfect for salads; flat green Continental lentils or massor dhal lentils from India are also good. Chunks of crumbly feta or a mild goat's milk cheese provide a colour and flavour contrast, but cubes of hard cheese are also inviting.

1 Drain the lentils and place them in a large pan. Pour in plenty of cold water and add the onion and bay leaf. Bring to the boil, boil hard for 10 minutes, then lower the heat and simmer for 20 minutes or according to the instructions on the packet.

2 Drain the lentils, discard the bay leaf and tip them into a bowl. Add salt and pepper to taste. Toss with the olive oil. Set aside to cool, then mix with the fresh parsley, oregano or marjoram and cherry tomatoes.

3 Add the cheese. Line a serving dish with chicory or frisée leaves and pile the salad in the centre. Scatter over the pine nuts and garnish with fresh herbs.

200g/7oz/scant 1 cup lentils (preferably Puy lentils), soaked for about 3 hours in cold water to cover
1 red onion, chopped
1 bay leaf
60ml/4 tbsp extra virgin olive oil
45ml/3 tbsp chopped fresh parsley
30ml/2 tbsp chopped fresh oregano or marjoram
250g/9oz cherry tomatoes, halved
250g/9oz feta, goat's cheese or Caerphilly cheese, crumbled
salt and ground black pepper
leaves of chicory (Belgian endive) or frisée and fresh herbs, to garnish
30–45ml/2–3 tbsp lightly toasted pine nuts, to serve

SERVES 6

3 celery sticks, thinly sliced
1 small onion, thinly sliced
1 carrot, coarsely grated
400g/14oz white cabbage
1 tart apple
2.5ml/1/2 tsp caraway seeds
50g/2oz/1/2 cup chopped walnuts
200g/7oz Cheddar or other hard
cheese, cut into small cubes

FOR THE DRESSING
45ml/3 tbsp olive oil
30ml/2 tbsp sunflower oil
45ml/3 tbsp cider vinegar or white
wine vinegar
generous pinch of sugar
generous pinch of mustard powder
generous pinch of dried tarragon
salt and ground black pepper

SERVES 6

WALDORF SALAD WITH CHEESE

—

A multi-purpose salad that can serve as a side dish or a vegetarian main course. The salad is best made the night before, so that it can marinate and soften before serving.

1 Put the celery, onion and carrot in a bowl. Cut the cabbage in quarters, remove and discard the core, then shred each piece finely. Add the cabbage to the bowl. Grate the apple coarsely and add it to the bowl along with the caraway seeds and walnuts. Toss well.

2 Whisk the dressing ingredients in a jug and season well with salt and pepper. Stir the dressing into the vegetable mixture and leave for at least 1 hour, preferably overnight, to allow the flavours to blend together. Mix in the cubes of cheese, then spoon into a dish and serve at once.

VARIATIONS
For a colour contrast, try making this salad with red cabbage or a mixture of red and white cabbage. Substitute toasted hazelnuts for the walnuts, if you like.

4 just-ripe pears
50g/2oz piece of Parmesan cheese
watercress, to garnish
water biscuits (crackers) or rye
bread, to serve (optional)

FOR THE DRESSING
30ml/2 tbsp extra virgin olive oil
15ml/1 tbsp sunflower oil
30ml/2 tbsp cider vinegar or white
wine vinegar
2.5ml/1/2 tsp soft light brown sugar
good pinch of dried thyme
15ml/1 tbsp poppy seeds
salt and ground black pepper
water biscuits or rye bread to
serve (optional)

SERVES 4

PEAR AND PARMESAN SALAD WITH POPPY SEED DRESSING

—

This is a good starter when pears are at their seasonal best. Try Packhams, Bartletts or Comice when plentiful, drizzled with a poppy-seed dressing and topped with shavings of Parmesan.

1 Cut the pears in quarters and remove the cores. Cut each pear quarter in half lengthways and arrange them on four small serving plates. Peel the pears if you wish, though they look more attractive unpeeled.

2 Make the dressing. Mix the oils, vinegar, sugar, thyme and seasoning in a pitcher. Whisk well, then tip in the poppy seeds. Trickle the dressing over the pears. Garnish with watercress and shave Parmesan over the top. Serve with water biscuits or thinly sliced rye bread, if you like.

VARIATION
Blue cheeses and pears also have a natural affinity. Stilton, Dolcelatte, Gorgonzola or Danish Blue (Danablu) are good substitutes. Allow about 200g/7oz and cut into wedges or cubes.

POTATO GRATIN WITH MUNSTER CHEESE

500g/1¼lb potatoes
150g/5oz Munster cheese, rind removed, and diced
60ml/4 tbsp double (heavy) cream
150ml/¼ pint/⅔ cup milk
30ml/2 tbsp snipped fresh chives or chopped fresh parsley
freshly grated nutmeg
salt and ground black pepper

SERVES 4

> **VARIATION**
> Any semi-soft or washed rinded French cheese can be used for this dish. Reblochon gives excellent results. For an extra-punchy flavour try Langes or Epoisses.

Munster melted in cream creates a superb topping for layered potatoes.

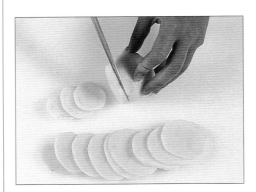

1 Peel the potatoes and slice them thinly. Cook the slices in boiling lightly salted water for about 10 minutes until tender. Drain and place in a gratin dish. Preheat the grill.

2 Mix the cheese, cream and milk in a small pan. Heat gently until the cheese has melted. Do not allow to boil. Remove from the heat, stir in the chives or parsley, add nutmeg to taste and season lightly. Pour the mixture over the potatoes. Grill until the topping is golden brown and serve.

PARSNIP, CARROT AND GOAT'S MILK CHEESE FRICASSÉE

4 parsnips
4 carrots
1 red onion, sliced
30ml/2 tbsp pine nuts or flaked almonds, lightly toasted
sprigs of tarragon, to garnish

FOR THE SAUCE
40g/1½oz/3 tbsp butter
40g/1½oz/⅓ cup plain (all-purpose) flour
300ml/½ pint/1¼ cups milk
130g/4½oz chèvre (goat's cheese)
15ml/1 tbsp chopped fresh or 2.5ml/½ tsp dried tarragon
salt and ground black pepper

SERVES 4–6

This excellent vegetarian main course also makes a fine accompaniment for roast or grilled (broiled) meats or fish. Serve it with roast potatoes.

1 Cut the parsnips and carrots into sticks. Put them in a pan and add the onion. Season, cover with cold water and bring to the boil. Lower the heat and simmer for 10 minutes or until the vegetables are just tender. Drain, reserving 200ml/7fl oz/scant 1 cup of the cooking water. Put the vegetables in a dish and keep hot.

2 Make the sauce. Melt the butter in a clean pan and stir in the flour. Cook for 1 minute, stirring, then gradually whisk in the reserved vegetable water and the milk. Heat, whisking, until the sauce boils and thickens. Simmer gently for 2 minutes.

3 Remove from the heat and stir in the chèvre, tarragon and salt and pepper. Pour the sauce over the vegetables and sprinkle with the pine nuts or almonds. Garnish with tarragon and serve.

Try other goat's milk cheeses, such as Chevrotin or chèvre-fevrille.

ROAST MEDITERRANEAN VEGETABLES WITH PECORINO

1 aubergine (eggplant), sliced
2 courgettes (zucchinni), sliced
2 (bell) peppers, red or yellow or one
of each, cored and quartered
1 large onion, thickly sliced
2 large carrots, cut in sticks
4 firm plum tomatoes, halved
extra virgin olive oil
45ml/3 tbsp chopped fresh parsley
45ml/3 tbsp pine nuts, lightly toasted
125g/4oz piece of Pecorino cheese
salt and ground black pepper
crusty bread, to serve (optional)

SERVES 4–6

VARIATION
Any hard sheep's milk cheese can be
used for the topping. Try Spanish
Manchego or British Malvern.

Aubergines, courgettes, peppers and tomatoes make a marvellous medley when roasted and served drizzled with fragrant olive oil. Shavings of sheep's milk Pecorino add the perfect finishing touch.

1 Layer the aubergine slices in a colander, sprinkling each layer with a little salt. Leave to drain over a sink or plate for about 20 minutes, then rinse thoroughly, drain well and pat dry with kitchen paper. Preheat the oven to 220°C/425°F/Gas 7.

2 Spread out the vegetables in one or two large roasting tins (pans). Brush the vegetables lightly with olive oil and roast them in the oven for about 20 minutes or until they are lightly browned and the skins on the peppers have begun to blister.

3 Transfer the vegetables to a large serving platter. If you like, peel the peppers. Trickle over any vegetable juices from the pan and season with salt and pepper. As the vegetables cool, sprinkle them with more oil (preferably extra virgin olive oil). When they are at room temperature, mix in the parsley and pine nuts.

4 Using a vegetable peeler, shave the Pecorino and scatter the shavings over the vegetables. Serve with crusty bread as a starter or an accompaniment for a buffet or barbecue.

CAULIFLOWER AND BROCCOLI MORNAY

As we become more aware of the value of simple, honest flavours, this nursery favourite is enjoying a revival. The secret of a good cheese sauce is not to make it too thick and to stir in the cheese off the heat so that it melts gently.

1 medium cauliflower
2 heads of broccoli
1 onion, sliced
3 hard-boiled eggs, quartered
6 cherry tomatoes, halved (optional)
30–45ml/2–3 tbsp breadcrumbs

FOR THE SAUCE
40g/1¹/₂oz/3 tbsp butter
40g/1¹/₂oz/¹/₃ cup plain
(all purpose) flour
600ml/1 pint/2¹/₂ cups milk or a
mixture of milk and vegetable water
150g/5oz/1¹/₄ cups grated mature
(aged) Cheddar cheese
freshly grated nutmeg
salt and ground black pepper

SERVES 4–6

VARIATIONS
The sauce can also be used for Macaroni Cheese. Cook 200g/7oz/ 1³/₄ cups dried macaroni or pasta shapes according to the package instructions. Add 1 sliced onion when boiling the macaroni, if desired. Drain and mix with the sauce, quartered hard-boiled eggs and tomato halves.

Use any mature hard cheese suitable for cooking. Red Leicester gives the sauce a deep golden colour. For a more pungent flavour, try a Munster.

To make a quick cheese sauce, melt 250g/9oz/2¹/₄ cups grated mature Cheddar into 475ml/16fl oz/2 cups scalded single (light) cream. Season. Flavour with freshly grated nutmeg.

1 Trim the cauliflower and broccoli and cut them into even-size florets, slicing the thinner parts of the stalks if you prefer. Bring a large pan of lightly salted water to the boil and cook the cauliflower, broccoli and onion slices for 5–7 minutes or until just tender. Do not over-cook.

2 Drain, reserving some of the vegetable water if you intend using it for the sauce. Place the vegetables in a shallow heatproof dish and add the quartered eggs.

3 To make the sauce, melt the butter in a pan and stir in the flour. Cook for 1 minute.

4 Gradually add the milk, or milk and vegetable water, whisking constantly until it boils to a thick and smooth sauce. Lower the heat and simmer for 2 minutes until glossy. Remove from the heat and whisk three-quarters of the cheese into the sauce and season with nutmeg, salt and pepper.

5 Preheat the grill (broiler). Pour the sauce over the vegetables and dot with the tomato halves, if using. Mix the remaining cheese with the dried breadcrumbs. Sprinkle the mixture over the vegetables, and grill until the top is bubbling and golden brown, then serve immediately.

MAIN MEAL DISHES

There are meals when cheese is a good complementary ingredient to meat or fish.

In the main, it is a good idea to use cheese that does not overpower the rest of the ingredients,

but sometimes a strong cheese works very well: for instance, a piquant blue cheese is

delicious with veal, and only the best full-flavoured Greek Kefalotiri cheese will do for a

truly memorable Moussaka.

VEAL WITH SMOKED CHEESE SAUCE

Sheep's milk cheeses melted with cream make a simple and luxurious sauce for serving with pan-fried veal escalopes or chops. The escalopes are used as purchased, not beaten thin as for schnitzel.

25g/1oz/2 tbsp butter
15ml/1 tbsp extra virgin
olive oil
8 small veal escalopes (scallops)
2 garlic cloves, crushed
250g/9oz/2¼ cups button (white)
mushrooms or closed cup
mushrooms, sliced
125g/4oz/1 cup frozen peas, thawed
60ml/4 tbsp/¼ cup brandy
250ml/8fl oz/1 cup whipping cream
150g/5oz Idiazabal (smoked sheep's
milk cheese) or Manchego, diced
salt and ground black pepper
sprigs of flat leaf parsley,
to garnish

SERVES 4

VARIATION
This dish would also work well with lean pork steaks. However, as it is important to ensure that pork is well cooked right through, they will need a longer frying time.

1 Melt half the butter with the oil in a large heavy-based frying pan. Season the escalopes with plenty of pepper and brown them in batches on each side over a high heat. Reduce the heat and cook for about 5 minutes on each side until just done. The escalopes should feel firm to the touch, with a very light springiness.

2 Lift the escalopes on to a serving dish and keep hot. Add the remaining butter to the pan. When it melts, stir-fry the garlic and mushrooms for about 3 minutes.

3 Add the peas, pour in the brandy and cook until all the pan juices have been absorbed. Season lightly.

4 Using a slotted spoon, remove the mushrooms and peas and place on top of the escalopes. Pour the cream into the pan and stir in the diced cheese. Heat gently until the cheese has melted. Season with pepper only and pour over the escalopes and vegetables. Serve immediately, garnished with sprigs of flat leaf parsley.

POLPETTINI WITH FONTINA

Meatballs are easy to stuff with nuggets of creamy cheese that melt during cooking. In this Italian dish, the meatballs are filled with Fontina cubes and then rolled in crumbs and fried.

500g/1¼lb lean minced (ground) beef
500g/1¼lb lean minced pork
3 garlic cloves, crushed
grated rind and juice of 1 lemon
2 slices of day-old bread, crumbed
*40g/1½oz/½ cup freshly grated
Parmesan cheese*
2.5ml/½ tsp ground cinnamon
5ml/1 tsp dried oregano
2 eggs, beaten
5ml/1 tsp salt
*150g/5oz Fontina cheese,
cut into 16 cubes*
*115–150g/4–5oz/1–1¼ cups natural-
coloured dried breadcrumbs*
olive oil, for shallow frying
ground black pepper
*fresh herbs and freshly grated
Parmesan, to garnish*
*cooked pasta, a mixed leaf salad and
tomato sauce, to serve*

SERVES 6–8

VARIATION
Use cubes of raclette, Gouda or
Monterey Jack instead of Fontina.

1 Preheat the oven to 180°C/350°F/ Gas 4. Put the minced beef and pork with the garlic, lemon rind and juice, fresh breadcrumbs, Parmesan, cinnamon and oregano in a bowl. Stir in the beaten eggs and beat well. Add the salt and a generous grinding of black pepper.

2 Using clean hands occasionally dipped into cold water, knead the mixture to ensure all the ingredients are well distributed, then shape it into 16 balls. Cup each ball in turn in your hand and press a piece of Fontina into the centre. Reshape the ball, making sure the cheese is well covered.

3 Roll the meatballs in the dried crumbs. Heat the olive oil in a large frying pan. Add the meatballs in batches and cook them quickly all over until lightly browned and sealed. Transfer them to a roasting tin (pan) and bake for 20 minutes or until cooked through. Garnish with fresh herbs and Parmesan and serve with pasta, salad and tomato sauce.

MOUSSAKA

Although feta is perhaps their best-known cheese, the Greeks have a number of others that can be used in cooking. Kefalotiri, a hard cheese made with sheep's or goat's milk, makes the perfect topping for a classic Moussaka.

2 large aubergines (eggplants),
45ml/3 tbsp olive oil
675g/1½lb lean minced (ground) beef
1 onion, chopped
2 garlic cloves, crushed
2 large fresh tomatoes, chopped, or
200g/7oz canned chopped tomatoes
120ml/4fl oz/½ cup dry white wine
45ml/3 tbsp chopped fresh parsley
45ml/3 tbsp fresh breadcrumbs
2 egg whites
salt and ground black pepper

FOR THE TOPPING
40g/1½oz/3 tbsp butter
40g/1½oz/⅓ cup plain (all-purpose) flour
400ml/14fl oz/1⅔ cups milk
2.5ml/½ tsp freshly grated nutmeg
150g/5oz/1¼ cups grated Kefalotiri
2 egg yolks, plus 1 whole egg

SERVES 6

1 Slice thinly and layer the aubergines in a colander, sprinkling each layer with salt. Drain for 20 minutes, then rinse and pat dry with kitchen paper.

2 Preheat the oven to 190°C/375°F/ Gas 5. Spread out the aubergines in a roasting tin (pan). Brush them with olive oil, then bake for 10 minutes until just softened. Remove and cool. Leave the oven on.

3 Make the meat sauce. Heat the olive oil in a large pan and brown the minced beef, stirring frequently. When the meat is no longer pink and looks crumbly, add the onion and garlic and cook for 5 minutes.

4 Add the chopped fresh or canned tomatoes to the pan and stir in the wine. Season with plenty of salt and pepper to taste.

5 Bring to the boil, then lower the heat, cover and simmer for 15 minutes. Remove the pan from the heat, leave to cool for about 10 minutes, then stir in the chopped parsley, fresh bread-crumbs and egg whites.

VARIATION
Use sliced par-boiled potatoes instead of the aubergines and substitute grated mature Cheddar or Gruyère for the Kefalotiri.

6 Lightly grease a large baking dish, then spread out half the sliced aubergines in an even layer on the base. Spoon over the meat sauce, spread it evenly, then top with the remaining aubergines.

7 To make the topping, put the butter, flour and milk in a pan. Bring to the boil over a low heat, whisking all the time until the mixture thickens to form a smooth, creamy sauce. Lower the heat and simmer for 2 minutes. Remove the pan from the heat, season, then stir in the nutmeg and half the cheese.

8 Cool for 5 minutes, then beat in the egg yolks and the whole egg. Pour the sauce over the aubergine topping and sprinkle with the remaining cheese. Bake for 30–40 minutes or until golden brown. Allow the dish to stand for 10 minutes before serving.

VEAL SCALOPPINE WITH ANCHOVIES AND MOZZARELLA

50g/2oz/¼ cup unsalted butter
50g/2oz can anchovies
4 fresh tomatoes, peeled and chopped
30ml/2 tbsp chopped fresh flat leaf parsley
6 veal escalopes (scallops), about 100g/3¾oz each
200g/7oz mozzarella cheese, cut in thin slices
30ml/2 tbsp olive oil
175ml/6fl oz/¾ cup Marsala or medium dry sherry
30–45ml/2–3 tbsp whipping cream
salt and ground black pepper
fresh herbs, to garnish
cooked pasta, to serve

SERVES 6

Scaloppine are thin escalopes of veal cut across the grain from the top rump so that they hold their shape while cooking. For this Italian dish, they are rolled around a filling of anchovies, tomatoes and mozzarella before being pan fried and served with a rich Marsala sauce.

VARIATIONS
Try smoked mozzarella or Provolone or Bel Paese instead of regular mozzarella. If you prefer not to eat veal, substitute thinly sliced pork escalopes or turkey steaks.

1 Melt half the butter in a small pan. Drain the anchovies and add them to the pan. Cook gently, stirring with a wooden spoon, until they break down to a pulp. Stir in the tomatoes and cook for about 5 minutes until they have softened and reduced. Tip into a bowl, cool, then stir in the parsley.

2 Place each veal escalope in turn between two sheets of baking parchment and beat with a mallet or rolling pin until thin. Spread the escalopes out on a board and sprinkle with ground black pepper. Divide the anchovy and tomato mixture among them, leaving the edges free.

3 Top with the slices of cheese. Fold the long edges of each escalope towards the centre, then bring up the sides to form a neat parcel. Secure with kitchen string or cocktail sticks.

4 Heat the remaining butter with the oil in a frying pan. Brown the rolled escalopes, in batches if necessary, then pour in the Marsala or sherry. Cook, uncovered, for 5 minutes or until the the Marsala or sherry has reduced and thickened. Transfer the rolls to a serving plate, stir the pan juices to incorporate any sediment, then pour in the cream. Reheat without boiling, then strain over the rolls. Garnish with fresh herbs and serve with pasta.

CHICKEN CORDON BLEU

A classic that is perennially popular, this consists of chicken breats stuffed with smoked ham and Gruyère, then coated in egg and breadcrumbs and fried until golden.

1 Slit the chicken breasts about three-quarters of the way through, then open them up and lay them flat. Place a slice of ham on each cut side of the chicken, trimming to fit if necessary so that the ham does not hang over the edge.

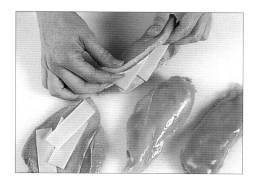

2 Top with the Gruyère slices, making sure that they are well within the ham slices. Fold over the chicken and reshape, pressing well to seal and ensuring that no cheese is visible.

3 Spoon the flour for coating into a shallow bowl. Pour the beaten eggs into another shallow bowl and mix the breadcrumbs with the thyme and seasoning in a third bowl. Toss each stuffed breast in the flour, then coat in egg and breadcrumbs, shaking off any excess. Lay the crumbed breasts flat on a plate, cover and chill for at least 1 hour in the fridge to set the coating.

4 To cook, heat the butter and oil in a frying pan. When the fat stops foaming, gently slide in the coated breasts, two at a time. Shallow fry over a medium-low heat for about 5 minutes each side, turning over carefully with a fish slice (spatula). Drain on kitchen paper and keep hot while you cook the remaining breasts. Serve with a side salad.

4 skinless, boneless chicken breast portions, about 130g/4¹/₂oz each
4 very thin smoked ham slices, halved and rind removed
about 90g/3¹/₂oz Gruyère cheese, thinly sliced
plain (all-purpose) flour, for coating
2 eggs, beaten
75g/3oz/³/₄ cup natural-coloured dried breadcrumbs
5ml/1 tsp dried thyme
40g/1¹/₂oz/3 tbsp butter
30ml/2 tbsp olive oil
salt and ground black pepper
mixed leaf side salad, to serve

SERVES 4

VARIATION
Instead of Gruyère, try one of the herb-flavoured hard cheeses, such as Double Gloucester with Chives.

FRENCH ROAST CHICKEN WITH COMTÉ CHEESE

Comté is excellent for cooking as it melts easily to a creamy, glossy texture with a good flavour. To make this French dish, you will need a large flameproof casserole plus a shallow ovenproof serving dish.

75g/3oz/6 tbsp butter
30ml/2 tbsp sunflower oil
1.75kg/4–4¹/₂lb roasting chicken
3 carrots, sliced in rings
2 leeks, sliced
2 celery sticks, sliced
1 litre/1³/₄ pints/4 cups chicken stock or water
300ml/¹/₂ pint/1¹/₄ cups dry white wine
4 sprigs of thyme
250g/9oz/2¹/₄ cups button mushrooms, halved
30ml/2 tbsp plain (all-purpose) flour
150ml/¹/₄ pint/²/₃ cup crème fraîche or double (heavy) cream
1 egg yolk
30ml/2 tbsp fresh lemon juice
freshly grated nutmeg
125g/4oz/1 cup grated Comté cheese
salt and ground black pepper

SERVES 6

1 Heat a third of the butter with the oil in a large flameproof casserole. Add the chicken and turn it in the fat until it is golden brown. Remove and set aside.

2 Add the vegetables to the casserole. Sauté gently for 5 minutes, then place the bird on top. Pour in the stock or water and the wine, with 1 sprig of thyme. Season well, bring to the boil, then lower the heat and cover the casserole. Simmer very gently for about 1 hour or until the chicken is cooked though.

3 Meanwhile, melt half the remaining butter in a small pan and stir-fry the mushrooms for 2–3 minutes. Do not allow them to soften or they will give up their liquid. Lift them out with a slotted spoon and set them aside. Mix the last of the butter with the flour to make a paste. Set this aside too.

4 Preheat the oven to 220°C/425°F/ Gas 7. Put the cream in a jug and stir in the egg yolk and lemon juice, with nutmeg to taste.

5 Transfer the cooked chicken to a shallow heatproof dish and cover with tented foil. Remove the sprig of thyme from the casserole and discard it.

6 Return the casserole to the heat and boil rapidly until the liquid has reduced by half, then purée the stock and vegetables together in a blender or food processor. Scrape the purée back into the casserole, return to a gentle simmer and gradually whisk in knobs of the butter-and-flour paste until the sauce has thickened and is smooth. Remove from the heat again and slowly whisk in the cream mixture.

7 Surround the chicken with the mushrooms. Press half the cheese on to the chicken breast, trickle the sauce over and sprinkle over the rest of the cheese. Bake for about 15 minutes or until the cheese is golden brown. Garnish with the remaining thyme sprigs and serve.

SALMON KEDGEREE, FRENCH-STYLE

This all-in-one supper dish is ideal for informal entertaining as it can be made ahead of time and reheated for about half an hour before being served with a tossed salad.

1 Put the salmon in a wide, shallow pan. Add the bay leaf and parsley stalks, with salt and pepper. Pour in the water and poach the fish for about 12 minutes until just tender. Lift out the fish, discard the herbs and pour the liquid into a pan. Leave the fish to cool, then remove any bones and flake the flesh.

2 Add the rice to the pan containing the fish poaching liquid. Bring the liquid to the boil, then lower the heat, cover and simmer for 10 minutes without lifting the lid. Remove the pan from the heat and allow the rice to stand undisturbed for 5 minutes.

3 Meanwhile, make the sauce. Mix the milk, flour and butter in a pan. Bring to the boil over a low heat, whisking constantly until the sauce is smooth and thick. Stir in the curry paste or mustard, with salt and pepper to taste. Simmer for 2 minutes.

4 Preheat the grill (broiler). Remove the sauce from the heat and stir in the chopped parsley and rice, with half the cheese. Using a large metal spoon, fold in the flaked fish and eggs. Spoon into a shallow gratin dish and sprinkle with the rest of the cheese. Heat under the grill until the topping is golden brown and bubbling.

> **VARIATIONS**
> Prawns (shrimp) could be substituted for the salmon and Lancashire or Mahon could be used instead of Cheddar. The dish also works well with pasta shapes instead of rice.

675g/1½lb fresh salmon fillet, skinned
1 bay leaf
a few parsley stalks
1 litre/1¾ pints/4 cups water
400g/14oz/2 cups basmati rice
30–45ml/2–3 tbsp chopped fresh parsley
175g/6oz/1½ cups grated Cheddar cheese
3 hard-boiled eggs, chopped
salt and ground black pepper

FOR THE SAUCE
1 litre/1¾ pints/4 cups milk
40g/1½oz/⅓ cup plain (all-purpose) flour
40g/1½oz/3 tbsp butter
5ml/1 tsp mild curry paste or Dijon mustard

SERVES 6

STEAK WITH ROQUEFORT AND WALNUT BUTTER

Make up a roll of savoury blue cheese butter to keep in the fridge to top steaks. This is also good served on pork chops.

2 shallots, chopped
75g/3oz/6 tbsp butter,
slightly softened
150g/5oz Roquefort cheese
30ml/2 tbsp finely chopped walnuts
15ml/1 tbsp finely snipped
fresh chives
15ml/1 tbsp olive oil or
sunflower oil
4 lean rump (round) steaks, about
125g/4oz each
120ml/4fl oz/1/2 cup dry white wine
30ml/2 tbsp crème fraîche or
double (heavy) cream
salt and ground black pepper
fresh chives, to garnish
runner (green) beans, to serve

SERVES 4

1 Sauté the shallots in a third of the butter. Tip into a bowl and add half the remaining butter, the cheese, walnuts, snipped chives and pepper to taste. Chill lightly, roll in foil to a sausage shape and chill again until firm.

2 Heat the remaining butter with the oil in a heavy frying pan and cook the steaks for about 3 minutes each side, or until cooked to your liking. Season the steaks and remove them from the pan.

3 Pour the wine into the pan and stir to incorporate any sediment. Bubble up for a minute or two, then stir in the crème fraîche or cream. Season and pour over the steaks. Cut pats of the Roquefort butter from the roll and put one on top of each steak. Garnish with chives. Lightly cooked runner beans make the ideal accompaniment.

PAN-ROASTED COD WITH A VERMOUTH AND CHÈVRE SAUCE

—

Team chunky white cod with a quick pan sauce of vermouth and a light, creamy chèvre sauce. Tomatoes grilled (broiled) with herbs add colour.

4 pieces of cod fillet, about 150g/5oz each, skinned
30ml/2 tbsp olive oil
4 spring onions (scallions), chopped
150ml/¹/4 pint/²/3 cup dry vermouth, preferably Noilly Prat
300ml/¹/2 pint/1¹/4 cups fish stock
45ml/3 tbsp crème fraîche or double (heavy) cream
65g/2¹/2 oz chèvre (goat's cheese), rind removed, and chopped
30ml/2 tbsp chopped fresh parsley
15ml/1 tbsp chopped fresh chervil
salt and ground black pepper
grilled plum tomatoes, to serve
flat leaf parsley, to garnish

SERVES 4

VARIATION
Instead of cod you could use salmon, haddock or plaice. The cooking time may change according to the thickness of the fish fillets.

1 Remove any stray bones from the cod fillets. Rinse the fish under cold running water and pat dry with kitchen paper. Place the pieces on a plate and season generously with salt and pepper.

2 Heat a non-stick frying pan, then add 15ml/1 tbsp of the oil, swirling it around to coat the bottom. Add the pieces of cod and cook, without turning or moving them, for 4 minutes or until nicely caramelized. Turn each piece over and cook the other side for a further 3 minutes or until just firm. Remove it to a serving plate and keep hot.

3 Heat the remaining oil and stir-fry the spring onions for 1 minute. Add the vermouth and cook until reduced by half. Add the stock and cook again until reduced by half. Stir in the cream and chèvre and simmer for 3 minutes. Add salt and pepper, stir in the herbs and spoon over the fish. Garnish with parsley and serve with grilled tomatoes.

VEGETARIAN DISHES

Since cheese is a fairly rich protein food, many classic cheese dishes are also vegetarian. Some of the best come from Italy: Aubergine Parmigiana, risotto flavoured with Parmesan, crisp risotto fritters with nuggets of mozzarella inside, and polenta cooked with Gorgonzola. There are also classic recipes for a cheese soufflé, an omelette and a fabulous fondue, and Twice-baked Spinach and Cheese Roulade – a superb dinner-party dish.

AUBERGINE PARMIGIANA

—

A classic Italian dish, in which blissfully tender sliced aubergines are layered with melting creamy mozzarella, fresh Parmesan and a good home-made tomato sauce.

3 medium aubergines (eggplant), thinly sliced
olive oil, for brushing
300g/11oz mozzarella cheese, sliced
125g/4oz/1⅓ cups freshly grated Parmesan cheese
30–45ml/2–3 tbsp breadcrumbs
basil sprigs, to garnish
salt and ground black pepper

FOR THE SAUCE
30ml/2 tbsp olive oil
1 onion, finely chopped
2 garlic cloves, crushed
400g/14oz can chopped tomatoes
5ml/1 tsp sugar
about 6 basil leaves

SERVES 4–6

1 Layer the aubergine slices in a colander, sprinkling each layer with a little salt. Drain over a sink for about 20 minutes, then rinse thoroughy under cold running water and pat dry with kitchen paper.

2 Preheat the oven to 200°C/400°F/ Gas 6. Lay the aubergine slices on non-stick baking sheets, brush the tops with olive oil and bake for 10–15 minutes until softened.

3 Make the sauce. Heat the oil in a pan and sauté the onion and garlic for 5 minutes. Add the canned tomatoes and sugar, with salt and pepper to taste. Bring to the boil, then lower the heat and simmer for about 10 minutes until reduced and thickened. Tear the basil leaves into small pieces and add them to the sauce.

4 Layer the aubergines in a greased shallow ovenproof dish with the sliced mozzarella, the tomato sauce and the grated Parmesan, ending with a layer of Parmesan mixed with the bread-crumbs. Bake for 20–25 minutes until golden brown and bubbling. Allow to stand for 5 minutes before cutting. Serve garnished with basil.

MALFATTI WITH ROASTED PEPPER SAUCE

The Italians use their rich but light cream cheese – ricotta – in sweet and savoury dishes. This recipe has it beaten into deliciously light spinach dumplings, called malfatti, served with a smoky pepper and tomato sauce.

*500g/1¹/4lb young leaf spinach
1 onion, finely chopped
1 garlic clove, crushed
15ml/1 tbsp extra virgin
olive oil
350g/12oz/1¹/2 cups ricotta cheese
3 eggs, beaten
50g/2oz/¹/2 cup breadcrumbs
50g/2oz/¹/2 cup plain
(all-purpose) flour
50g/2oz/²/3 cup freshly grated
Parmesan cheese
freshly grated nutmeg
25g/1oz/2 tbsp butter, melted
salt and ground black pepper*

*FOR THE SAUCE
2 red (bell) peppers, quartered
and cored
30ml/2 tbsp extra virgin
olive oil
1 onion, chopped
400g/14oz can chopped tomatoes
150ml/¹/4 pint/²/3 cup water*

SERVES 4

1 Make the sauce. Preheat the grill (broiler) and grill the pepper quarters skin side up until they blister and blacken. Cool slightly, then peel and chop. Heat the oil in a pan and lightly sauté the onion and peppers for 5 minutes. Add the tomatoes and water, with salt and pepper to taste. Bring to the boil, lower the heat and simmer gently for 15 minutes. Purée in a food processor or blender, then return to the clean pan and set aside.

2 Trim any thick stalks from the spinach, wash it well if necessary, then blanch in a pan of boiling water for about 1 minute. Drain, refresh under cold water and drain again. Squeeze dry, then chop finely.

3 Put the finely chopped onion, garlic, olive oil, ricotta, eggs and breadcrumbs in a bowl. Add the spinach and mix well. Stir in the flour and 5ml/1 tsp salt with half the Parmesan, then season to taste with pepper and nutmeg.

4 Roll the mixture into 16 small logs and chill lightly.

5 Bring a large pan of water to the boil. Carefully drop in the malfatti in batches and cook for 5 minutes. Remove with a fish slice (spatula) and toss with the melted butter. To serve, reheat the sauce and divide it among four plates. Arrange four malfatti on each and sprinkle over the remaining Parmesan. Serve at once.

PEPPERS WITH RICE, FETA AND PINE NUT STUFFING

4 large red, green or yellow (bell) peppers, or a mixture
475ml/16fl oz/2 cups vegetable stock
200g/7oz/1 cup long grain rice
30ml/2 tbsp olive oil
1 onion, chopped
2 garlic cloves, crushed
125g/4oz/1 cup button (white) mushrooms, chopped
1 carrot, grated
4 tomatoes, chopped
15ml/1 tbsp chopped fresh dill
90g/3¹/₂oz feta cheese, crumbled
75g/3oz/1 cup pine nuts, lightly toasted
30ml/2 tbsp currants
25g/1oz/¹/₃ cup freshly grated Parmesan cheese
salt and ground black pepper
salad of mixed leaves, to serve

SERVES 4

A popular family supper dish, which can be prepared ahead and reheated. Serve it with a cheese sauce for a delicious change.

1 Preheat the oven to 190°C/375°F/ Gas 5. Cut the peppers in half lengthways and remove the cores and seeds. Bring a large pan of water to the boil, add the peppers and blanch for 5 minutes. Remove from the pan using a slotted spoon. Leave to drain upside down, then place, hollow up, in a lightly greased baking dish.

Any strong-flavoured Cheddar (right) could be used in place of the feta. Or try fresh chèvre instead.

2 Put the stock in another pan. Tip in the rice and bring to the boil, then lower the heat. Cover the pan and simmer gently for 15 minutes. Remove the pan from the heat without lifting the lid and leave to stand in a warm place for 5 minutes.

3 Meanwhile, heat the olive oil and sauté the onion and garlic for 5 minutes. Stir in the mushrooms, carrot and tomatoes with salt and pepper to taste. Cover, cook for a further 5 minutes until softened, then mix in the rice, dill, feta, pine nuts and currants.

4 Divide the mixture among the pepper halves, sprinkle over the Parmesan and bake for 20 minutes or until the topping has browned.
Serve with a mixed salad.

SEMOLINA AND PESTO GNOCCHI

These gnocchi are cooked rounds of semolina dough, which are brushed with melted butter, topped with cheese and baked. When carefully cooked, they taste wonderful with a home-made tomato sauce.

1 Heat the milk in a large non-stick pan. When it is on the point of boiling, sprinkle in the semolina, stirring constantly until the mixture is smooth and very thick. Lower the heat and simmer for 2 minutes.

2 Remove from the heat and stir in the pesto and sun-dried tomatoes, with half the butter and half the Pecorino. Add the eggs, with nutmeg, salt and pepper to taste. Spoon on to a clean shallow baking dish or tin (pan) to a depth of 1cm/½ in and level the surface. Leave to cool, then chill.

VARIATIONS
Substitute any mature hard grating cheese for the Pecorino, such as the Spanish cheeses Manchego or Mahon. Instead of pesto, use a small pack of chopped frozen spinach that has been thawed and squeezed of excess water or 90ml/6 tbsp mixed chopped herbs.

3 Preheat the oven to 190°C/375°F/ Gas 5. Lightly grease a shallow baking dish. Using a 4cm/1½in scone (round) cutter, stamp out as many rounds as possible from the semolina pasta.

4 Place the leftover semolina paste on the base of the greased dish and arrange the rounds on top in overlapping circles. Melt the remaining butter and brush it over the gnocchi. Sprinkle over the remaining Pecorino. Bake for 30–40 minutes until golden. Serve with tomato sauce and garnish with basil.

750ml/1¼ pints/3 cups milk
200g/7oz/generous 1 cup semolina
45ml/3 tbsp pesto sauce
60ml/4 tbsp finely chopped
sun-dried tomatoes, patted dry
if oily
50g/2oz/¼ cup butter
75g/3oz/1 cup freshly grated
Pecorino cheese
2 eggs, beaten
freshly grated nutmeg
salt and ground black pepper
tomato sauce, to serve
basil, to garnish

SERVES 4–6

PORCINI AND PARMESAN RISOTTO

The success of a good risotto depends on the quality of the rice used and the technique. For this variation of the classic risotto alla milanese, saffron, porcini mushrooms and Parmesan are stirred into the creamy cooked rice.

10g/¼oz/2 tbsp dried porcini mushrooms
300ml/½ pint/1¼ cups warm water
1.2 litres/2 pints/5 cups vegetable stock
generous pinch of saffron threads
30ml/2 tbsp olive oil
1 onion, finely chopped
1 garlic clove, crushed
250g/9oz/1¼ cups arborio or carnaroli rice
150ml/¼ pint/⅔ cup dry white wine or 45ml/3 tbsp dry vermouth
25g/1oz/2 tbsp butter
50g/2oz/⅔ cup freshly grated Parmesan cheese
salt and ground black pepper

SERVES 4

VARIATIONS
There are endless variations on this delectable dish. The proportion of stock to rice, onions, garlic and butter must remain constant but you can ring the changes with the flavourings and cheese. Try Pecorino with lightly blanched baby vegetables for Risotto Primavera. Chopped bacon and peas make the famous risi e bisi.

1 Soak the dried mushrooms in the warm water for 20 minutes. Lift out with a slotted spoon. Filter the soaking water through a layer of kitchen paper in a sieve, then place it in a pan with the stock. Bring the liquid to a gentle simmer.

2 Put about 45ml/3 tbsp of the hot stock in a cup and stir in the saffron strands. Set aside.

3 Finely chop the mushrooms. Heat the oil in a separate pan and lightly sauté the onion, garlic and mushrooms for 5 minutes. Gradually add the rice, stirring. Cook for 2 minutes, stirring. Season with salt and pepper.

4 Pour in the wine or vermouth. Cook, stirring, until it has been absorbed, then ladle in a quarter of the stock. Bring to the boil, stirring. Cook until most of the liquid has been absorbed.

5 Continue to add the stock a ladle at a time, stirring after each addition. The secret of good risotto is to add the stock gradually and to stir frequently to encourage a creamy texture from the starch grains.

6 After about 20 minutes, when all the stock has been absorbed and the rice is cooked but still has a "bite", stir in the butter, saffron water and strands and half the Parmesan. Serve, sprinkled with the remaining Parmesan.

Pecorino makes a good alternative to Parmesan in this risotto.

SUPPLI AL TELEFONO

*45ml/3 tbsp finely chopped
fresh parsley
1 quantity Porcini and Parmesan
Risotto (see page 52), made without
the saffron
200g/7oz mozzarella cheese, cut into
20 cubes
2 eggs, beaten
150g/5oz/1¼ cups breadcrumbs
corn or vegetable oil, for
deep frying
fresh herbs, to garnish*

MAKES 20

VARIATION
For the filling, use cubes of Emmental,
Provolone or even Monterey Jack
instead of mozzarella.

*These are risotto fritters with nuggets of mozzarella inside. When bitten into,
the cheese is drawn out in thin strings, like telephone wires, hence the name.*

1 Stir the parsley into the risotto,
cool, then chill until firm. Divide into
20 portions and shape each into a ball.
Press a cube of cheese into each ball of
rice and reshape neatly. Coat the rice
balls in the beaten egg, then the breadcrumbs, and chill again for 30 minutes
to set the coating.

2 Heat the oil for deep frying to 180°C/
350°F. Cook about five fritters at a time
for 3–5 minutes until golden brown and
crisp. Drain the fritters on kitchen
paper and keep warm on an uncovered
plate in a warm oven so that the
coating remains crisp. Garnish with
fresh herbs and serve immediately.

CHILLI CHEESE TORTILLA WITH FRESH TOMATO SALSA

Good warm or cold, this is like a quiche without the pastry base. Cheese and chillies are more than a match for each other.

45ml/3 tbsp sunflower or olive oil
1 small onion, thinly sliced
2–3 fresh green jalapeño
chillies, sliced
200g/7oz cold cooked potato,
thinly sliced
120g/4¹/₄oz/generous 1 cup grated
Manchego, Mexican queso blanco or
Monterey Jack cheese
6 eggs, beaten
salt and ground black pepper
fresh herbs, to garnish

FOR THE SALSA
500g/1¹/₄lb fresh tomatoes, peeled,
seeded and finely chopped
1 fresh mild green chilli, seeded and
finely chopped
2 garlic cloves, crushed
45ml/3 tbsp chopped fresh
coriander (cilantro)
juice of 1 lime
2.5ml/¹/₂ tsp salt

SERVES 4

COOK'S TIP
If you like, you can brown the tortilla
top under a grill (broiler), using a
frying pan with a flameproof handle.

1 Make the salsa. Put the tomatoes in a bowl and add the chopped chilli, garlic, coriander, lime juice and salt and pepper. Mix well and set aside.

2 Heat half the oil in a large omelette pan and gently fry the onion and jalapeños for 5 minutes, stirring once or twice, until softened. Add the potato and cook for a further 5 minutes until lightly browned, taking care to keep the slices whole.

3 Using a slotted spoon, transfer the vegetables to a warm plate. Wipe the pan with kitchen paper, then pour in the remaining oil. Heat well and return the vegetable mixture to the pan. Scatter the cheese over the top.

4 Pour in the beaten egg, making sure that it seeps under the vegetables. Cook the tortilla over a gentle heat until set. Serve in wedges, garnished with fresh herbs, with the salsa on the side.

POLENTA WITH GORGONZOLA AND WILD MUSHROOM SAUCE

Like semolina gnocchi, polenta is made with a ground cereal — cornmeal. After it is cooked and thickened, creamy Gorgonzola is stirred in and the mixture is left to set before being cut into wedges and grilled (broiled).

900ml/1¹/₂ pints/3³/₄ cups milk
900ml/1¹/₂ pints/3³/₄ cups water
5ml/1 tsp salt
300g/11oz/generous 2 cups polenta
50g/2oz/¹/₄ cup butter
125g/4oz Gorgonzola cheese
sprigs of thyme, to garnish

FOR THE SAUCE
40g/1¹/₂oz dried porcini mushrooms, soaked in 150ml/¹/₄ pint/²/₃ cup hot water for 15 minutes
25g/1oz/2 tbsp butter
125g/4oz/1 cup button (white) mushrooms, chopped
60ml/4 tbsp dry white wine
generous pinch of dried thyme
60ml/4 tbsp mascarpone cheese
salt and ground black pepper

SERVES 4–6

1 Pour the milk and water into a large heavy pan. Add the salt and bring to the boil. Using a long-handled spoon, stir the liquid briskly with one hand while drizzling in the polenta with the other. When the mixture is thick and smooth, lower the heat to a gentle simmer and cook for about 20 minutes, stirring occasionally.

2 Remove from the heat and stir in the butter and Gorgonzola. Spoon the polenta into a shallow dish, level the surface and cool. Let the polenta set until solid, then cut into wedges.

3 Meanwhile, make the sauce. Drain the porcini, reserve the soaking liquid. Finely chop the porcini and strain the liquid through a sieve lined with kitchen paper.

4 Melt half the butter in a small pan. Sauté the chopped fresh mushrooms for about 5 minutes. Add the wine, porcini and strained soaking liquid, with the dried thyme. Season to taste. Cook for 2 minutes more. Stir in the mascarpone and simmer for a few minutes, until reduced by a third. Set the sauce aside to cool.

5 Grill (broil) the polenta pieces on a pre-heated, ridged grill pan until crisp. Melt the remaining butter and brush it over the polenta. Serve hot, with the cooled sauce. Garnish with thyme.

TWICE-BAKED SPINACH AND GOAT'S MILK CHEESE ROULADE

A roulade is rather like a Swiss (jelly) roll soufflé. Because it has air trapped inside, it magically rises again on reheating and becomes quite crisp on the outside. This is an impressive dinner-party dish.

300ml/1/2 pint/11/4 cups milk
50g/2oz/1/2 cup plain
(all-purpose) flour
150g/5oz/2/3 cup butter
100g/33/4oz chèvre (goat's cheese),
chopped
40g/11/2oz/1/2 cup freshly grated
Parmesan cheese, plus extra
for dusting
4 eggs, separated
250g/9oz/21/4 cups fresh shiitake
mushrooms, sliced
275g/10oz young spinach leaves
45ml/3 tbsp crème fraîche or
fromage frais
salt and ground black pepper

SERVES 4

1 Preheat the oven to 190°C/375°F/Gas 5. Line a 30 × 20cm/12 × 8in tin with baking parchment, making sure that the paper rises well above the sides of the tin. Lightly grease.

2 Mix together the milk, flour and 50g/2oz/1/4 cup of the butter in a large pan. Bring to the boil over a low heat, whisking until thick and creamy. Lower the heat and simmer for 2 minutes, then mix in the chèvre and half the Parmesan. Cool for 5 minutes, then beat in the egg yolks and plenty of salt and pepper.

3 Whisk the egg whites in a grease-free bowl until soft peaks form. Carefully fold the whites into the chèvre mixture, using a large metal spoon. Spoon the mixture into the prepared tin, spread gently to level, then bake for 15–17 minutes until the top feels just firm.

4 Let the roulade cool for a few minutes, then invert it on to a sheet of baking parchment dusted with Parmesan. Carefully tear off the lining paper in strips. Roll the roulade up in the baking parchment and leave to cool completely.

5 Make the filling. Melt the remaining butter and set aside 30ml/2 tbsp. Add the mushrooms to the pan and stir-fry for 3 minutes. Stir in the spinach and drain well, then add the crème fraîche or fromage frais. Season, then cool.

6 Preheat the oven to the original temperature. Unroll the roulade and spread over the filling. Roll it up again and place, join side down, in a baking dish. Brush with the reserved melted butter and sprinkle with the remaining Parmesan. Bake for 15 minutes or until risen and golden. Serve immediately.

CLASSIC CHEESE SOUFFLÉ

At its simplest, a soufflé is merely a thick sauce with beaten egg whites folded in – not at all difficult to achieve, especially if the base is made ahead and the whites added just before baking. Timing is the only ticklish area, as a soufflé waits for no one.

50g/2oz/¼ cup butter
30–45ml/2–3 tbsp breadcrumbs
200ml/7fl oz/scant 1 cup milk
30g/1¼oz/3 tbsp plain (all-purpose) flour
pinch of cayenne pepper
2.5ml/½ tsp curry paste or mustard or freshly grated nutmeg
50g/2oz/½ cup grated mature (aged) Cheddar cheese
25g/1oz/⅓ cup freshly grated Parmesan cheese
4 eggs, separated, plus 1 extra egg white
salt and ground black pepper

SERVES 2–3

1 Preheat the oven to 190°C/375°F/Gas 5. Melt 15ml/1 tbsp of the butter and grease a 1.2 litre/2 pint/5 cup soufflé dish. Coat the inside of the dish evenly with the breadcrumbs.

2 Put the milk in a large pan. Add the remaining butter, flour and cayenne, with the curry paste, mustard or nutmeg. Bring to the boil over a low heat, whisking steadily until the mixture thickens to a smooth sauce.

3 Simmer the sauce for a minute or two, then turn off the heat and whisk in all the Cheddar and half the Parmesan. Cool a little, then beat in the egg yolks and check the seasoning. The mixture should be well seasoned.

4 Whisk all the egg whites in a large grease-free bowl until they form soft, glossy peaks. Do not overbeat or the whites will become grainy and difficult to fold in.

VARIATIONS

Crumbled blue cheese, such as Stilton or Shropshire Blue or Fourme d'Ambert, make delicious flavourings. For a more substantial soufflé, put a chopped vegetable mixture, such as ratatouille or sautéed mushrooms, on the bottom of the dish before adding the cheese mixture and baking as above.

5 Spoon some of the beaten egg whites into the sauce to lighten it. Beat well, then scrape the rest of the whites into the pan and, using a figure-of-eight movement, carefully fold them into the mixture with a large metal spoon.

6 Pour the mixture into the prepared dish, level the top and place the dish on a baking sheet. Sprinkle on the remaining Parmesan. Bake for 20–25 minutes until risen and golden. Serve.

Stilton makes a delicious flavouring for a soufflé.

CLASSIC CHEESE OMELETTE

Perhaps the ultimate fast food – a couple of eggs, some nicely flavoured cheese, a little butter and a good pan and you have a full and satisfying meal within minutes. Technique is important with omelettes. The centre should be soft and the cheese just melted and creamy.

2 large (US extra large) eggs
15ml/1 tbsp chopped fresh herbs,
such as chives, parsley or dill
a knob (pat) of unsalted
(sweet) butter
50g/2oz/¹/₂ cup grated cheese, such
as Gruyère, Gouda or Cheddar
salt and ground black pepper
flat leaf parsley, to garnish
tomato wedges, to serve

SERVES 1

VARIATIONS
You can add ingredients to the cheese. Crunchy garlicky croûtons are good, as are sautéed sliced mushrooms and chopped tomatoes. As for the cheese, this is a good time to experiment.

2 Heat the butter in the pan. Pour in the beaten eggs, swirling the pan so that the mixture coats the base. Using a fork or spatula, pull the cooked areas of egg away from the pan sides, letting the uncooked egg run in to fill the space. When the egg at the sides is firm, but the centre still soft, scatter over the cheese.

1 Heat a 20cm/8in heavy-based omelette pan or non-stick frying pan. Break the eggs into a bowl and beat in the herbs and seasoning. It is not necessary to add water or milk, which would only dilute the egg.

3 Allow to cook undisturbed for about 30 seconds, then fold the edge of the omelette nearest the handle over a third. Roll the omelette over on to a warmed plate. Serve immediately, with tomato wedges and a garnish of flat leaf parsley.

POTATO AND CHEESE CAKE

This dish appears in many guises, cheese and potatoes having a natural affinity. Choose a hard, well-flavoured cheese – in France, where it is called Truffade, this cake would be made with a Tomme or Cantal. In England, Cheddar would be used, and the dish would be called Pan Haggarty.

a little sunflower oil or
melted butter
675g/1¹/₂lb potatoes, peeled and
very thinly sliced
1 large onion, thinly sliced
150g/5oz/1¹/₄ cups grated hard
cheese, such as mature Cheddar,
Tomme or Cantal
freshly grated nutmeg
salt and ground black pepper
mixed salad leaves,
to garnish

SERVES 4–6

VARIATION
In France, a non-vegetarian version of this dish is cooked with diced streaky (fatty) bacon and the cheese is chopped. The ingredients are mixed and cooked slowly in a little lard in a pan on top of the stove.

1 Preheat the oven to 190°C/375°F/ Gas 5. Lightly grease the base of a shallow baking dish or roasting tin (pan) with the oil or melted butter.

2 Layer the potato, onion and cheese in the dish, brushing the potatoes with oil or butter and seasoning with nutmeg, salt and pepper. Finish with a layer of cheese. Bake for 45 minutes, or until golden brown. Leave to stand for about 5 minutes, then serve in wedges, with a salad garnish.

MIXED VEGETABLE FRITTATA

*45ml/3 tbsp olive oil
1 red onion, thinly sliced
1 large red (bell) pepper, cored and thinly sliced
1 large yellow (bell) pepper, cored and thinly sliced
2 garlic cloves, crushed
1 medium courgette (zucchini), thinly sliced
6 eggs
150g/5oz Fontina, Provolone or Taleggio cheese, grated
salt and ground black pepper
dressed mixed salad leaves, to garnish*

SERVES 4

Eggs, cheese and vegetables form the basis of this excellent supper dish. Served cold, in wedges, it makes tasty picnic fare too.

1 Heat 30ml/2 tbsp of the oil in a large heavy frying pan. Fry the onion and pepper slices over a low heat for about 10 minutes until softened.

2 Add the remaining oil to the pan. When it is hot, tip in the garlic and courgette slices and fry for 5 minutes, stirring constantly.

3 Beat the eggs with salt and pepper in a bowl. Mix in the cheese.

4 Pour the egg and cheese mixture over the vegetables, stirring lightly to mix. Make sure that the base of the pan is evenly covered with egg. Cook over a low heat until the mixture is just set. Traditionally, a frittata is inverted on to a plate and returned to the pan upside-down to cook the top, but it may be easier to brown the top lightly under a hot grill for a few minutes (protect the pan handle, if necessary).

5 Allow the frittata to stand in the pan for about 5 minutes before cutting. This is delicious served hot or cold, with a salad garnish.

FONDUE

A fondue is simply a mixture of melted cheeses with wine to keep it liquid. Flavourless starch prevents the cheeses from separating, while garlic and Kirsch add extra flavour.

1 Rub the inside of a *caquelon* (traditional fondue pan) or deep flameproof pan with the cut side of the garlic halves. If you like, you can then chop the garlic finely and place it in the pan.

2 Mix the arrowroot or potato starch with 30ml/2 tbsp of the wine in a small bowl. Set aside. Pour the rest of the wine into the pan.

3 Heat the wine very slowly. Add about a third of the sliced or grated cheese, and continue heating the mixture, stirring until the cheese starts to melt and the liquid to bubble.

4 Slowly stir in the arrowroot or potato starch mixture, then the rest of the cheese, a little at a time. Add the Kirsch and pepper. Place the fondue over a candle warmer on the table, with cubes of bread for dipping.

1 fat garlic clove, halved
5ml/1 tsp arrowroot or potato starch
300ml/¹/₂ pint/1¹/₄ cups dry white wine
3 × 350g/12oz portions hard, melting cheese (see Cook's Tip), thinly sliced or coarsely grated
45–60ml/3–4 tbsp Kirsch
ground black pepper
cubes of country-style bread, for dipping

SERVES 6

COOK'S TIP
In Switzerland the cheese mixture would comprise Emmental, Gruyère and Appenzeller or raclette, while the French favour Comte or Beaufort.

PASTRIES, PIZZAS AND PASTA

Many of the world's great street foods rely on cheese. Because it melts so easily, either over direct heat or in the most rustic oven, it is ideal for slicing on to a pizza or wrapping between sheets of filo pastry. There are also dozens of cheesy pasta dishes, where the cheese is tossed into hot pasta or layered to make a mouthwatering lasagne. This sort of food is ideal for feeding crowds with speed and without fuss.

BOREK

Versions of these crisp, cheese-filled pastries, are a common feature of street food throughout much of the Mediterranean. They are easy to make at home, but require a little time and patience.

250g/9oz feta cheese, crumbled
2.5ml/¹/₂ tsp freshly grated nutmeg
30ml/2 tbsp each chopped fresh parsley, dill and mint
10 filo pastry sheets, each about 30 × 18cm/12 × 7in
75g/3oz/6 tbsp melted butter or 90ml/6 tbsp olive oil
ground black pepper

MAKES 10

COOK'S TIPS

When using filo pastry, it is important to keep unused sheets covered so that they don't dry out. The quantities for filo pastry in the recipe above are approximate, as the size of filo sheets varies. Any unused pastry will keep in the fridge for a week or so, if it is well wrapped.

1 Preheat the oven to 190°C/375°F/Gas 5. Mix the feta, nutmeg and herbs in a bowl. Add pepper to taste and mix to a creamy filling.

2 Brush a sheet of filo lightly with butter or oil, place another on top of it and brush that too.

3 Cut the buttered sheets in half lengthways to make 10 strips, each 30 × 9cm/12 × 3¹/₂ in. Place 5ml/1 tsp of the cheese filling at the base of a long strip, fold the corners in diagonally to enclose it, then roll the pastry up into a cigar shape.

4 Brush the end with a little butter or oil to seal, then place join side down on a non-stick baking sheet. Repeat with the remaining pastry and filling. Brush the borek with more butter or oil and bake for 20 minutes or until crisp and golden. Cool on a wire rack and serve at room temperature.

RATATOUILLE AND FONTINA STRUDEL

Mix a colourful jumble of ratatouille vegetables with chunks of creamy Fontina or Bel Paese, then wrap in sheets of filo and bake for a delicious, summery party pastry.

*1 small aubergine (eggplant), diced
45ml/3 tbsp extra virgin olive oil
1 onion, sliced
2 garlic cloves, crushed
1 red (bell) pepper, cored and sliced
1 yellow (bell) pepper, cored and sliced
2 courgettes (zucchini), cut into small chunks
generous pinch of dried mixed herbs
30ml/2 tbsp pine nuts
30ml/2 tbsp raisins
8 filo pastry sheets, each about 30 × 18cm/12 × 7in
50g/2oz/¼ cup butter, melted
130g/4½oz/generous 1 cup Fontina or Bel Paese cheese, cut into small cubes
salt and ground black pepper
dressed mixed salad, to serve*

SERVES 6

VARIATION
Port Salut, a soft French Tomme or a Caerphilly can be used instead of Fontina or Bel Paese.

1 Layer the diced aubergine in a colander, sprinkling each layer with salt. Drain over a sink for 20 minutes, then rinse and pat dry.

2 Heat the oil in a large frying pan and gently fry the onion, garlic, peppers and aubergine for about 10 minutes.

3 Add the courgettes, herbs and salt and pepper. Cook for 5 minutes, until softened. Cool to room temperature, then stir in the pine nuts and raisins.

4 Preheat the oven to 180°C/350°F/ Gas 4. To assemble the strudel, brush two sheets of filo pastry lightly with a little of the melted butter. Lay the filo sheets side by side, overlapping them by about 5cm/2in, to make a large rectangle. Cover with the remaining filo, in the same way, brushing each layer with a little of the melted butter. Save some butter for the top. Spoon the vegetable mixture down one long side of the filo.

5 Scatter the cheese over, then roll up to a long sausage. Transfer the roll to a non-stick baking sheet, curling it round in a circle. Brush with the remaining melted butter and bake for 30 minutes, until golden. Cool for 10 minutes, before slicing. Serve with mixed salad.

CHEESE AND ONION QUICHE

Perfect for picnics, parties or family suppers, this quiche celebrates a timeless combination: cheese and onion. Omit the bacon, if you prefer.

*200g/7oz/1³/₄ cups plain
(all-purpose) flour
2.5ml/¹/₂ tsp salt
90g/3¹/₂oz/scant ¹/₂ cup butter or
sunflower margarine*

*FOR THE FILLING
25g/1oz/2 tbsp butter
1 large onion, thinly sliced
4 rindless streaky (fatty) bacon,
chopped (optional)
3 eggs
300ml/¹/₂ pint/1¹/₄ cups crème
fraîche, single (light) cream or milk
1.5ml/¹/₄ tsp freshly grated nutmeg
90g/3¹/₂oz mature (aged) Cheddar,
Gruyère or Manchego cheese, grated
salt and ground black pepper*

SERVES 6–8

1 Make the pastry. Sift the flour and salt into a bowl. Rub in the fat until the mixture resembles fine crumbs. Trickle in enough water to make a firm dough, about 60ml/4 tbsp. Knead the dough lightly until smooth, wrap in clear film and chill for 20 minutes.

2 Roll out the dough on a lightly floured surface and line a 23cm/9in flan tin (tart pan) with a removable base. Press the pastry well into the sides and let it rise above the rim by about 1cm/¹/₂in to allow for shrinkage. Prick the pastry base a few times.

3 Line the flan tin with foil and either baking beans, uncooked rice or pie weights and chill again for about 15 minutes. Preheat the oven to 200°C/400°F/Gas 6. Place a baking sheet in the oven. Stand the flan tin on the sheet and bake "blind" for 15 minutes. Remove the weight and foil and return the pastry to the oven for a further 5 minutes at 180°C/350°F/Gas 4.

4 Make the filling. Melt the butter in a pan and sauté the onion and bacon, if using, for 10 minutes. In a bowl, beat the eggs and crème fraîche, cream or milk. Add the nutmeg and seasoning.

5 Spoon the onion mixture into the cooked pastry case and scatter over the cheese. Pour the egg and cream liquid slowly over the filling, making sure none spills over the edge of the pastry case. Place the quiche in the oven and cook for 35–40 minutes or until the filling has just set. Remove from the oven, leave to cool, then gently ease the quiche out of the tin and place it on a plate for serving.

CALZONE

Looking like a folded pizza, a calzone consists of bread dough wrapped around a cheese and vegetable filling. The traditional tomato and garlic can be enlivened with chunks of sweet melting cheese, olives, crumbled grilled bacon, slices of pepperoni or chorizo or anchovy fillets.

30ml/2 tbsp extra virgin
olive oil
1 small red onion,
thinly sliced
2 garlic cloves, crushed
400g/14oz can chopped tomatoes
50g/2oz sliced chorizo sausage
50g/2oz/1/2 cup pitted black olives
500g/1 1/4lb bread dough mix
200g/7oz mozzarella or other
semi-soft cheese, diced
5ml/1 tsp dried oregano
salt and ground black pepper
oregano sprigs, to garnish

MAKES 4

VARIATION
Mozzarella is the classic pizza cheese, but you may wish to experiment with other semi-soft melting cheeses, such as Fontina or Provolone.

1 Heat the oil in a frying pan and sauté the onion and garlic for 5 minutes. Add the tomatoes and cook for 5 minutes more or until slightly reduced. Add the chorizo and olives. Season well.

2 Make up the dough mix according to the instructions on the packet. Cover the bowl and leave the dough to rise until it has doubled in bulk.

3 Knock back the risen dough and divide it into four portions. Roll out each portion of dough to a circle measuring about 20cm/8in. Preheat the oven to 200°C/400°F/Gas 6. Lightly grease two baking sheets.

4 Spread the filling on half of each dough circle, leaving a margin around the edge. Scatter over the cheese.

5 Sprinkle the filling with the dried oregano. Dampen the edges of the dough with cold water. Fold the dough in half and press well to seal.

6 Place two calzones on each baking sheet. Bake for 12–15 minutes until golden. Cool for 2 minutes, then loosen with a palette knife, garnish with oregano and serve immediately.

CHICKEN, CHEESE AND LEEK JALOUSIE

1.5kg/3–3½lb roasted chicken
2 large leeks, thinly sliced
2 garlic cloves, crushed
40g/1½oz/3 tbsp butter
125g/4oz/1 cup button (white)
mushrooms, sliced
200g/7oz/scant 1 cup low-fat
cream cheese
grated rind of 1 small lemon
45ml/3 tbsp chopped fresh parsley
2 × 250g/9oz blocks puff pastry,
thawed if frozen
1 egg, beaten
salt and ground black pepper
fresh herbs, to garnish

SERVES 6

A jalousie is a family-size lattice pastry roll with a mild, creamy filling. Ready-made puff pastry and cooked chicken make this a good choice for informal entertaining.

1 Strip the meat from the chicken, discarding the skin and bones. Chop or shred the meat and set it aside.

2 Sauté the leeks and garlic in the butter for 10 minutes. Stir in the mushrooms and cook for 5 minutes. Leave to cool, then add the cream cheese, lemon rind, parsley and salt and pepper. When cold, stir in the chicken.

3 Stack the blocks of pastry on top of each other and roll out on a lightly floured work surface to a large rectangle, about 35 × 25cm/14 × 10in. Lop the pastry over a rolling pin and lift it on to a non-stick baking sheet.

4 Spoon the filling on to the pastry, leaving a generous margin at the top and the bottom, and 10cm/4in on each side. Cut the pastry sides diagonally up to the filling at 2cm/¾in intervals.

Try a creamy blue cheese, such as Dolcellate Torta, for this jalousie.

5 Brush the edges of the pastry with the beaten egg. Draw the pastry strips over each other in alternate crosses to "plait" ("braid") the pastry. Seal the top and bottom edges.

6 Glaze the jalousie with beaten egg. Allow it to rest while you preheat the oven to 200°C/400°F/Gas 6. Bake for 15 minutes, then lower the oven temperature to 190°C/375°F/Gas 5 and bake for a further 15 minutes, or until the pastry is golden brown and crisp.

7 Allow the jalousie to stand for about 10 minutes before sliding it on to a board or platter to serve. Garnish with fresh herbs.

VARIATION
Chopped cooked ham can be used instead of chicken.

GOUGÈRE

*100g/3³/₄oz/scant 1 cup strong
plain (bread) flour
1.5ml/¹/₄ tsp salt
75g/3oz/6 tbsp cold butter, diced
200ml/7fl oz/scant 1 cup water
3 eggs, beaten
150g/5oz Emmental, mature (aged)
Cheddar or Gruyère cheese, grated*

*FOR THE FILLING
250g/9oz smoked haddock fillet
1 bay leaf
250ml/8fl oz/1 cup milk
40g/1¹/₂oz/3 tbsp butter
1 small red onion, chopped
150g/5oz/1¹/₄ cups mushrooms, sliced
5ml/1 tsp mild curry paste (optional)
25g/1oz/¹/₄ cup plain
(all-purpose) flour
generous squeeze of fresh
lemon juice
30ml/2 tbsp chopped fresh parsley
salt and ground black pepper*

SERVES 4

COOK'S TIP
Choose pale yellow, traditionally
smoked haddock rather than vividly
dyed, bright yellow fillets.

1 Lightly grease a shallow ovenproof
dish. Sift the flour and salt on to a
sheet of baking parchment. Place the
butter and water in a pan and heat
gently. As soon as the butter has
melted, bring the water to the boil.
Immediately tip in all the flour.

*Choux pastry is very easy to make. Add cubes of hard cheese, such as Gruyère
or Cheddar, and bake it in a dish with a lightly spiced haddock and
mushroom filling and you have an impressive supper dish.*

2 Beat the mixture until it comes away
from the sides of the pan. (It will look
alarmingly lumpy at first.) Remove
the pan from the heat and cool for
5 minutes – this is important.

3 Slowly work the beaten eggs into the
dough until the mixture has a good
dropping consistency and holds its
shape. You may not need all the egg.
Stir in two-thirds of the grated cheese.

4 Spoon the choux paste around the
edge of the prepared dish, making sure
it comes well up the sides. Set aside.
Choux paste can be made in advance
and kept chilled for about 24 hours.

VARIATIONS
For an alternative filling use cooked
chicken or ratatouille. Both the choux
paste and the filling can be flavoured
with blue cheese: use slightly less
than the quantity suggested in the
main recipe.

5 Preheat the oven to 180°C/350°F/
Gas 4. To make the filling, put the
haddock in a baking dish with the bay
leaf. Pour in the milk, cover and bake
for 15 minutes until just cooked. Lift
out the fish. Discard the bay leaf but
reserve the hot milk. Remove the skin
from the haddock and flake the flesh.

6 In a pan, melt the butter and sauté
the onion and mushrooms for
5 minutes. Mix in the curry paste, if
using, then add the flour. Gradually add
the hot milk, stirring until the sauce is
smooth. Simmer for about 2 minutes,
then add the lemon juice, parsley and
season to taste. Stir in the flaked fish.

7 Raise the oven temperature to
200°C/400°F/Gas 6. Spoon the filling
into the centre of the uncooked paste.
Sprinkle with the rest of the cheese.
Bake for 35–40 minutes until the
gougère has risen and is golden brown.
Serve immediately.

FOUR CHEESE CIABATTA PIZZA

1 loaf of ciabatta bread
1 garlic clove, halved
30–45ml/2–3 tbsp olive oil
about 90ml/6 tbsp passata or
sugocasa (pizza sauce)
1 small red onion, thinly sliced
30ml/2 tbsp chopped pitted olives
about 50g/2oz each of four cheeses,
one mature (Parmesan or Cheddar),
one blue-veined (Gorgonzola or
Stilton), one mild (Fontina or
Emmental) and a goat's cheese,
sliced, grated or crumbled
pine nuts or cumin seeds,
to sprinkle
salt and ground black pepper
sprigs of basil, to garnish

SERVES 2

Few dishes are as simple – or as satisfying – as this pizza made by topping a halved loaf of ciabatta.

1 Preheat the oven to 200°C/400°F/ Gas 6. Split the ciabatta bread in half. Rub the cut sides with the garlic, then brush over the oil. Spread with the passata or sugocasa, then add the onion slices and olives. Season.

2 Divide the cheeses between the ciabatta halves and sprinkle over the pine nuts or cumin seeds. Bake for 10–12 minutes, until bubbling and golden brown. Cut it into slices and serve immediately, garnished with basil.

CALIFORNIAN COURGETTE AND CHÈVRE PIZZA

Chefs from the US West Coast are adventurous when it comes to making pizzas. Their wood-burning ovens give bases and cheese toppings a delicious smoky flavour. Cook this tasty pizza at a high temperature to char the vegetables lightly. Dot with goat's milk cheese for an interesting tang.

1 large ready-made, good-quality, crisp pizza base
45ml/3 tbsp drained sun-dried tomatoes in oil
45ml/3 tbsp drained roasted (bell) peppers in oil
1 courgette (zucchini), thinly sliced
1 red onion, thinly sliced
250g/9oz young chèvre (goat's cheese), crumbled
15ml/1 tbsp chopped fresh oregano or marjoram
a little extra virgin olive oil, to drizzle
salt and ground black pepper
fresh herbs, to garnish

SERVES 2

VARIATIONS
A creamy, crumbly blue cheese such as Bleu d'Auvergne makes a good alternative to chèvre. A smoked mozzarella would also work well.

For a Greek flavour, try lightly sautéed aubergine (eggplant) slices in place of the courgettes and use feta rather than chèvre.

3 Bake the pizza for 10–12 minutes or until the cheese has melted and the vegetables have begun to char. Garnish with herbs and serve, cut into wedges.

Hard goat's milk cheese would be ideal – simply grate over the pizza.

1 Preheat the oven to 220°C/425°F/ Gas 7. Place the pizza base on a baking sheet. Chop the sun-dried tomatoes and peppers and spread them over the pizza base.

2 Scatter the slices of courgette and onion on top, then dot with the crumbled chèvre. Sprinkle with oregano or marjoram, season well and drizzle a little olive oil over the top.

LASAGNE AL FORNO

8–10 lasagne sheets, green or white
75g/3oz Parmesan cheese
salt and ground black pepper
sprigs of flat leaf parsley, to garnish

FOR THE MEAT SAUCE
45ml/3 tbsp olive oil
500g/1¼lb lean minced (ground) beef
75g/3oz smoked bacon or
pancetta, diced
130g/4½oz chicken livers, trimmed
and chopped (optional)
1 onion, finely chopped
2 garlic cloves, crushed
150ml/¼ pint/⅔ cup dry white
wine (optional)
30–45ml/2–3 tbsp tomato paste
2 × 400g/14oz cans chopped tomatoes
45ml/3 tbsp single (light)
cream (optional)

FOR THE WHITE SAUCE
600ml/1 pint/2½ cups milk
1 bay leaf
1 small onion, sliced
50g/2oz/¼ cup butter
40g/1½oz/⅓ cup plain (all-
purpose) flour
freshly grated nutmeg

SERVES 6

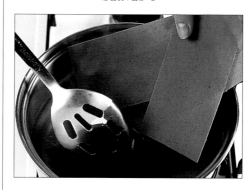

1 Bring a large pan of water to the boil and blanch the pasta sheets, a few at a time, for at least 2 minutes, taking care to keep them separate. Stir the pasta during cooking to stop it sticking. Drain the blanched sheets and set them aside in a bowl of cold water.

The classic lasagne is made with good home-made meat or ragù sauce and a white sauce or salsa besciamella layered with freshly grated Parmesan cheese. Keep the layers of sauces quite thin and don't make the lasagne too thick – the finished dish should hold its shape as you cut it.

2 Make the meat sauce. Heat the oil in a large frying pan and brown the minced beef. Add the bacon or pancetta and chicken livers, if using, and cook for 3–4 minutes. Add the onion and garlic, cook for 5 minutes more. Stir in the wine, if using. Cook until well reduced.

3 Stir in the tomato paste and tomatoes, with salt and pepper to taste. Bring to the boil, then lower the heat and simmer for 15–20 minutes until thickened. Stir in the cream, if using, and set aside.

4 While the meat sauce is simmering, make the white sauce. Pour the milk into a pan and add the bay leaf and sliced onion. Heat gently until the milk is just below boiling point, then remove the pan from the heat and leave to infuse for 10 minutes. Strain the milk into a jug and discard the bay leaf and onion.

5 Melt the butter in a pan and stir in the flour. Cook for 1 minute, stirring, then gradually whisk in the milk until the mixture boils and thickens to a smooth sauce. Season and add nutmeg to taste. Drain the pasta sheets and pat them dry with kitchen paper.

6 Spread some meat sauce on the base of a rectangular baking dish. Top with a layer of pasta sheets. Trickle over some white sauce and sprinkle with grated Parmesan. Repeat the layers until all the ingredients have been used. Finish with a layer made by swirling the last of the two sauces together. Sprinkle liberally with the remaining Parmesan.

7 Preheat the oven to 190°C/375°F/ Gas 5 and bake the lasagne for about 30 minutes until bubbling and golden brown. Allow to stand for 10 minutes before cutting. Serve garnished with flat leaf parsley.

NEW YORK-STYLE LASAGNE

This more sophisticated lasagne is made layering the meat sauce with ricotta cheese, spinach and sliced pepperoni or chorizo sausage. A mixture of minced beef and pork gives a good flavour.

about 8–10 lasagne sheets, green or white
400g/14oz fresh spinach
500g/1¼lb/2½ cups ricotta cheese
125g/4oz thinly sliced pepperoni or chorizo or kabanos sausage
50g/2oz/⅔ cup freshly grated Parmesan cheese
fresh herbs, to garnish

FOR THE MEAT SAUCE
30ml/2 tbsp olive oil
250g/9oz lean minced (ground) beef
250g/9oz lean minced (ground) pork
1 onion, chopped
2 garlic cloves, crushed
150ml/¼ pint/⅔ cup dry white wine or 60ml/4 tbsp dry vermouth
400g/14oz can chopped tomatoes
45ml/3 tbsp tomato purée (paste)
150ml/¼ pint/⅔ cup beef stock or water
2.5ml/½ tsp dried oregano
salt and ground black pepper

SERVES 6

1 Bring a large pan of water to the boil and blanch the pasta sheets, a few at a time, for at least 2 minutes, taking care to keep them separate. Stir the pasta during cooking to prevent it from sticking. Drain and set aside in a bowl of cold water.

2 Snap off any thick stalks from the spinach, then blanch the leaves in a pan containing a small amount of boiling water for 2 minutes, until just wilted. Drain the spinach and refresh under cold water. Drain again, then squeeze dry and chop the leaves.

3 Put the ricotta on a plate and break it up with a fork.

4 To make the meat sauce, heat the oil in a large frying pan, then add both types of mince and cook over a high heat for about 5 minutes, until well browned, stirring to break up any lumps. Add the onion and garlic and cook for 5 minutes more.

COOK'S TIP
Authentic Ricotta can sometimes be difficult to come by in more remote areas. However, it freezes well, so it is worth stocking up when you do locate a supply.

5 Pour the wine or vermouth into the frying pan and cook over a high heat until well reduced. Stir in the chopped tomatoes, tomato paste, beef stock or water and dried oregano, then season to taste with salt and pepper. Bring to the boil, then lower the heat and simmer gently uncovered for about 15 minutes until thickened.

6 Preheat the oven to 190°C/375°F/ Gas 5. In a large baking dish, layer the meat sauce with the lasagne sheets, chopped spinach and sliced sausage. Dot each layer of spinach and sausage with the ricotta and sprinkle with the Parmesan. Finish with a generous topping of Parmesan.

7 Bake the lasagne for 35–40 minutes until bubbling and golden brown. Allow to stand in a warm place for about 10 minutes before cutting and serving. Garnish with fresh herbs.

SPANAKOPITTA

This popular spinach and filo pastry pie comes from Greece. There are several ways of making it, but feta or Kefalotiri is inevitably included. Go easy on the seasoning as these cheeses are salty.

1kg/2¼lb fresh spinach
4 spring onions (scallion), chopped
300g/11oz feta or Kefalotiri cheese, crumbled or coarsely grated
2 large eggs, beaten
30ml/2 tbsp chopped fresh parsley
15ml/1 tbsp chopped fresh dill
45ml/3 tbsp currants (optional)
about 8 filo pastry sheets, each about 30 × 18cm/12 × 7in
150ml/¼ pint/⅔ cup olive oil
ground black pepper

SERVES 6

VARIATION

Graviera or Kasseri can be used instead of feta or Kefalotiri. A crumbly English cheese, such as Lancashire, also works well, even though it is not strictly authentic.

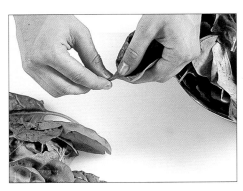

1 Preheat the oven to 190°C/375°F/ Gas 5. Break off any thick stalks from the spinach, then blanch the leaves in a pan containing a very small amount of boiling water for 1–2 minutes, until just wilted. Drain and refresh under cold water. Drain again, squeeze dry and chop roughly.

2 Place the spinach in a bowl with the spring onions and cheese, then pour in the eggs. Mix in the herbs and currants (if using). Season with pepper.

3 Brush a filo sheet with oil and fit it into a 23cm/9in pie dish (pan), allowing it to hang over the edges. Top with 3–4 more sheets; place these at different angles and brush each one with more oil, to make a roughly shaped pie case.

4 Spoon in the filling, then top with all but one of the remaining filo sheets. Brush each filo sheet with oil. Fold in the overhanging filo to seal in the filling. Brush the reserved filo with oil and scrunch it over the top of the pie.

5 Brush the pie with oil. Sprinkle with a little water to stop the filo edges from curling, then place on a baking sheet. Bake for about 40 minutes, until golden and crisp. Cool the pie for 15 minutes before serving.

PUMPKIN AND PARMESAN PASTA

The sweet flavour of pumpkins is nicely balanced by the mature flavour of Parmesan. Instead of being sprinkled on top of the pasta dish, this grated cheese is used in the sauce, and the crunch comes from garlic breadcrumbs.

1 Bring a large pan of water to the boil. Tip in the pumpkin cubes. Cook for about 10 minutes until just tender, then drain and set aside.

2 Melt two-thirds of the butter with the oil in a frying pan. Add the garlic and breadcrumbs. Fry gently until the crumbs are golden brown and crisp. Drain on kitchen paper and keep warm.

3 Cook the tagliatelle according to the packet instructions. Drain and set aside. Heat the remaining butter in a clean pan and fry the bacon and onion for 5 minutes. Stir in the cream and bring to just below boiling point. Add the pasta and reheat. Stir in the pumpkin, Parmesan, nutmeg, parsley, chives and seasoning. Serve sprinkled with garlic breadcrumbs and garnished with parsley.

800g/1³/₄lb fresh pumpkin flesh,
cut into small cubes
65g/2¹/₂oz/5 tbsp butter
15ml/1 tbsp olive oil
2 garlic cloves, crushed
75g/3oz/1¹/₂ cups breadcrumbs
300g/11oz tagliatelle
125g/4oz rindless smoked back
(lean) bacon, diced
1 onion, sliced
150ml/¹/₄ pint/²/₃ cup single
(light) cream
50g/2oz/²/₃ cup freshly grated
Parmesan cheese
freshly grated nutmeg
30ml/2 tbsp chopped fresh parsley
15ml/1 tbsp snipped fresh chives
salt and ground black pepper
sprigs of flat leaf parsley, to garnish

SERVES 4

CHEESE SAUCES FOR PASTA

Here are three quick and easy sauces – all using cheese – to toss with cooked pasta.
Each is sufficient for about 250g/9oz pasta strands or shapes.

MUSHROOM AND GORGONZOLA SAUCE

Gorgonzola melts easily with cream to make a delicious, quick sauce.

30ml/2 tbsp olive oil
250g/9oz/2¼ cups mushrooms, sliced
1 garlic clove, crushed
300ml/½ pint/1¼ cups single (light) cream
175g/6oz Gorgonzola cheese, rind removed, crumbled
salt and ground black pepper
15ml/1 tbsp chopped fresh parsley and 50g/2oz/½ cup chopped walnuts, to serve

1 Heat the olive oil in a pan and sauté the mushrooms for 5 minutes. Add the garlic and cook for 1–2 minutes more.

2 Stir in the cream, bring to the boil and cook for 1 minute. Stir in the Gorgonzola. Reheat gently to melt the cheese, but do not boil. Season and toss with cooked pasta. Serve at once, sprinkled with the parsley and walnuts.

HOME-MADE PESTO

The ideal no-cook pasta sauce, this is best made by hand with a pestle and mortar, although a food processor can be used if time is short. Use a mixture of Parmesan and Pecorino cheeses. Pine nuts are a recent addition and butter makes it enjoyably smooth.

75g/3oz/1½ cups fresh basil leaves, stalks removed
25g/1oz/2 tbsp pine nuts
2–3 garlic cloves, roughly chopped
125g/4oz/1⅓ cups mixed freshly grated Parmesan and Pecorino cheese
120ml/4fl oz/½ cup olive oil
25g/1oz/2 tbsp butter, softened
salt

1 Put the basil, pine nuts and garlic into a mortar. Add 2.5ml/½ tsp salt and grind with a pestle until the mixture forms a chunky paste.

2 Work in the cheeses until smooth. Beat the paste with a wooden spoon, gradually trickling in the olive oil as when making mayonnaise. Finally, beat in the butter.

3 Store pesto in a screw-top jar in the fridge. When you toss it into cooked pasta, thin it slightly, if you wish, by adding a little of the hot water used for cooking the pasta.

FONDUTA

This Italian answer to fondue is also used as a sauce for pasta, rice and polenta. If you can't find Fontina cheese, Gruyère will do.

400g/14oz Fontina cheese, cut into small cubes
250ml/8fl oz/1 cup creamy (half-and-half) milk
50g/2oz/¼ cup butter, cut into pieces
4 egg yolks
ground white pepper

1 Mix together the cheese and milk in a heavy pan or the top of a double boiler. Heat very gently on the hob or over simmering water, stirring frequently until the cheese has completely melted. Stir in the butter. The cheese will go into thin threads.

2 Beat the egg yolks in a large bowl with pepper. Pour the cheesy milk on to them, beating as you pour. Return the mixture to the clean pan and reheat very, very gently. Do not let the mixture boil or it will curdle. Pour over pasta, cooked rice or grilled polenta and eat quickly. The sauce is also good served solo, with chunks of bread to scoop it up.

OPPOSITE (FROM LEFT): Fonduta, Home-made Pesto and Mushroom and Gorgonzola Sauce.

DESSERTS

Fresh young cheeses like fromage frais, mascarpone and crème fraîche were created to be used in cooking or mixed with other ingredients. Their mild taste and slight astringency means that they are delicious sweetened with sugar or honey to make classic desserts such as Coeur à la Crème, Pashka, Sicilian Cassata, Tiramisù, delectable cheesecakes and a cream cheese-iced carrot cake.

REFRIGERATOR CHEESECAKE

200g/7oz/3¹/₂ cups digestive biscuits (graham crackers)
90g/3¹/₂oz/7 tbsp butter
15ml/1 tbsp golden (light corn) syrup
seasonal fruit and raspberry coulis, to serve
strawberry leaves, to decorate

FOR THE FILLING
grated rind and juice of 1 lemon
1 sachet powdered gelatine
200g/7oz/scant 1 cup low fat cream cheese, at room temperature
200g/7oz/scant 1 cup fromage frais or whipping cream
150g/5oz/²/₃ cup natural (plain) yogurt
50g/2oz/¹/₄ cup caster (superfine) sugar
5ml/1 tsp pure vanilla essence (extract)

SERVES 4–6

COOK'S TIP
The gelatine can be dissolved in a suitable bowl in the microwave. Follow the instructions on the packet.

This dessert is so simple, anyone could make it. Serve the cheesecake with seasonal fruits. In late summer, poached plums or apricots cooked in a spiced syrup are particularly good, although soft red berry fruits are also excellent. Make sure the cheese is at room temperature when you mix it.

1 Crush the biscuits to fine crumbs in a plastic food bag with a rolling pin, or using a food processor with a metal blade. Melt the butter and syrup in a pan, then mix with the crumbs.

2 Press the buttery crumbs into the base and up the sides of a 20cm/8in flan tin (tart pan) with a removable base. Chill for 1 hour.

3 Make the filling. Pour the lemon juice into a small heatproof dish and sprinkle the gelatine over. Leave the mixture until the gelatine absorbs the liquid and looks spongy, then place the dish in a large enough pan of barely simmering water and stir occasionally until the gelatine dissolves.

4 Mix the cheese and quark or fromage frais. Add the yogurt, lemon rind, sugar and vanilla. Beat until smooth, then beat some of the mixture into the dissolved gelatine. Add this to the cheesecake filling and beat well. Pour into the crumb crust and chill for 3 hours until set. Remove the cheesecake from the tin. Serve with fruit and raspberry coulis. Decorate with strawberry leaves.

VELVETY CHEESECAKE

The secret of a perfect baked cheesecake is to take as much care over the cooling as you do with the cooking. If you do not overbake the mixture, it will stay beautifully moist and will firm as it cools.

25cm/10in sponge cake
500g/1¼lb/2 cups cream cheese, softened
600ml/1 pint/2½ cups sour cream
200g/7oz/scant 1 cup caster (superfine) sugar
3 eggs, beaten
juice of 1 lemon
10ml/2 tsp pure vanilla essence (extract)
45–60ml/3–4 tbsp crushed digestive biscuit (graham cracker) crumbs
icing (confectioner's) sugar, to dust
fresh fruits, to serve

SERVES 6–8

VARIATIONS
Make the cheesecake without a base, if you prefer. If you like sultanas in your cheesecake, add a generous handful.

1 Preheat the oven to 160°C/325°F/ Gas 3. Lightly grease a 23cm/9in spring-form cake tin (pan). Using the base of the tin as a guide, cut out a round from the sponge cake and fit this into the tin. It should fit snugly, without any gaps.

4 Sprinkle the crushed biscuit crumbs evenly over the cheesecake and dust with a little sifted icing sugar. Serve with fresh fruits.

2 Mix the cream cheese, sour cream and sugar in a food processor. Process until smooth and creamy, then mix in the eggs, lemon juice and vanilla essence. Process briefly to blend.

3 Pour the filling on top of the sponge cake and level the surface. Bake for about 40 minutes, until the top is golden brown. Turn off the oven and leave the cake inside for another hour. Remove, allow the cake to cool to room temperature, then chill in the fridge overnight until firm. Run a table knife around the cheesecake and remove the sides of the tin. Slide a palette knife under the cake and lift it on to a serving plate.

250g/9oz/1 cup curd (farmer's) cheese
300ml/¹/2 pint/1¹/4 cups crème fraîche
or natural (plain) yogurt
30–45ml/2–3 tbsp vanilla-flavoured
caster (superfine) sugar
raspberry leaves, to decorate

FOR THE RASPBERRY COULIS
250g/9oz/1¹/2 cups fresh
raspberries, hulled
icing (confectioner's) sugar, to sweeten

MAKES 8

COOK'S TIP
If using ramekins, spoon the cheese mixture into a muslin-lined sieve set over a bowl. Leave to drain in the fridge for up to 2 days, then press into eight lightly greased ramekins. Turn out the moulded cheese immediately.

COEUR À LA CRÈME

This dessert is sheer simplicity – a curd cheese blended with crème fraîche, then sweetened and drained. Traditionally, perforated heart-shaped moulds are used, hence the name, but the mixture can be served in ramekins.

1 Beat the curd cheese and crème fraîche or natural yogurt in a bowl. Add vanilla sugar to taste.

2 Set eight traditional perforated moulds on a wire rack over a roasting pan. Spoon the cheese mixture into the moulds, filling each one to the brim.

3 Transfer the roasting pan to the refrigerator and leave the moulds to drain for up to 2 days.

4 To make the coulis, sieve the raspberries, then sweeten with icing sugar. Turn out the moulds and serve with the coulis, decorated with raspberry leaves.

---

2 eggs, separated, plus 2 egg yolks
90g/3¹/2oz/7 tbsp caster
(superfine) sugar
5ml/1 tsp vanilla essence (extract)
500g/1¹/4lb mascarpone cheese
250ml/8fl oz/1 cup freshly brewed
strong black coffee
60ml/4 tbsp rum or brandy
about 24 Italian Savoiardi or Boudoir
biscuits or ladyfingers
60ml/4 tbsp finely grated dark
(bittersweet) chocolate

SERVES 6–8

VARIATION
Dispense with the biscuit base, if you prefer, and serve the Tiramisù cream over a mixture of fresh, prepared summer fruit.

TIRAMISÙ

The Italians consider this the ultimate "pick-me-up", which is what the name means. It makes marvellous use of silky smooth mascarpone.

1 Whisk the egg yolks, sugar and vanilla in a heatproof bowl. Place over a pan of simmering water and whisk until the mixture is pale and thick and the whisk leaves a clear trail on the surface when lifted up. Remove the bowl from the pan and allow to cool, beating the mixture occasionally to prevent the formation of a skin.

2 When the mixture is cold, beat in the mascarpone. Whisk the egg whites in a large grease-free bowl until they form soft peaks, then carefully fold them into the mixture.

3 Mix the coffee and rum or brandy in a bowl. Dip the biscuits or ladyfingers quickly in the liquid, then arrange them in a glass dish. Spoon the mascarpone mixture over the top, then sprinkle with the grated chocolate. Chill for at least an hour before serving.

COOK'S TIP
If you prefer to avoid using uncooked egg whites, substitute albumen (egg white) powder.

LEMON CHEESE MOUSSE WITH BRANDY SNAP BASKETS

—

50g/2oz/1/4 cup butter
30ml/2 tbsp golden (light corn) syrup
50g/2oz/1/4 cup granulated sugar
grated rind and juice of 2 lemons
50g/2oz/1/2 cup plain (all-purpose) flour
1 orange, for shaping the biscuits
45ml/3 tbsp water
10ml/2 tsp powdered gelatine
250g/9oz/generous 1 cup curd
(farmer's) cheese
150ml/1/4 pint/2/3 cup natural
(plain) yogurt
30ml/2 tbsp clear honey
15ml/1 tbsp grated crystallized ginger
2 egg whites
mint sprigs, to decorate
selection of soft fruit, to serve
MAKES 6–8

COOK'S TIP

To save time, use purchased brandy snaps to make the baskets. Simply warm them in a low oven until they uncurl, then shape them over an orange. If the brandy snaps harden before you have a chance to shape them, then simply pop them back in the oven briefly to soften.

1 Make the baskets. Preheat the oven to 190°C/375°F/Gas 5. Line a large baking sheet with baking parchment. Melt the butter, syrup and sugar in a pan, then remove from the heat and stir in half the lemon rind and all the flour. Beat until smooth.

A delicious combination of a light cheesecake-style mousse with biscuit cups. Assemble the individual desserts at the last minute, so that they stay crisp.

2 Put about 30ml/2 tbsp of mixture on the prepared baking sheet. Using a small palette knife (metal spatula), spread out the mixture to a 13cm/5in circle. Add a second circle, some distance from the first to allow room for spreading. Bake for 5–7 minutes until the biscuits have spread out and are lacy and light golden brown.

3 Allow the biscuits to cool for about 1 minute to firm slightly, but not harden, then lift each in turn off the baking sheet using a palette knife. Gently press the biscuits over the orange, carefully fluting the edges, and protecting your hands with a clean dish towel, if necessary.

4 Remove the baskets when shaped and leave them to cool on a wire rack. Repeat the entire baking and shaping process with the remaining mixture until you have used it all.

5 Make the mousse. Pour the water into a bowl and sprinkle the gelatine over. Leave until spongy, then dissolve over a pan of simmering water.

6 Blend the cheese, yogurt, remaining lemon rind, lemon juice, honey and ginger in a food processor. Add the gelatine, blend briefly and pour into a bowl. Chill until just beginning to set.

7 Whisk the egg whites to soft peaks and fold into the mousse. Spoon into the baskets and serve, decorated with mint and accompanied by fruit.

SICILIAN CASSATA

Is this world-famous cheese dessert a chocolate-coated ice cream or a rum syrup-soaked cake? The answer is that it can be both, and a number of other variations too. Try to track down authentic Savoiardi biscuits as they hold their shape better than Boudoir biscuits or ladyfingers.

500g/1¼lb/2½ cups ricotta cheese
75g/3oz/¾ cup icing (confectioner's) sugar, plus extra for dusting
2.5ml/½ tsp vanilla essence (extract)
grated rind and juice of 1 orange
50g/2oz dark (bittersweet) chocolate, grated
250g/9oz/1½ cups mixed crystalized (candied) fruits, including orange, pineapple, citron, cherries and angelica
250ml/8fl oz/1 cup freshly brewed strong black coffee
120ml/4fl oz/½ cup rum
24 Savoiardi biscuits or ladyfingers
geranium leaves, to decorate

SERVES 8

1 Line the base and sides of a 20cm/8in round cake tin (pan) with clear film (plastic wrap). Put the ricotta in a bowl and sift in the sugar. Add the vanilla essence, orange rind and juice. Beat until smooth, then stir in the chocolate.

2 Cut the candied fruits into small pieces and stir into the ricotta.

3 Mix the coffee and rum in a bowl. Line the base of the tin with biscuits, dipping each biscuit in turn in the coffee mixture before fitting it in place. Cut the remaining biscuits in half, dip them in the liquid and arrange around the sides of the tin.

4 Spoon the cassata mixture into the centre and level the top. Cover with more clear film, then place a plate on top that exactly fits inside the rim of the tin. Weight this with a bag of dried beans or sugar, then chill overnight until firm.

5 Turn out to serve, shaking the tin firmly if necessary and tugging the clear film gently. Dust with a little sifted icing sugar and serve in wedges, decorated with geranium leaves.

PASHKA

This traditional Russian Easter dessert is made with curd (famer's) cheese and served with slices of kulich, a sweet yeast bread. The cheese mixture is pressed into a muslin (cheesecloth) -lined wooden mould to drain whey out, leaving a rich and delectably creamy mousse.

500g/1 1/4 lb/2 1/2 cups curd (farmer's) cheese, at room temperature
130g/4 1/2 oz/9 tbsp butter, softened
2 large egg yolks, optional
125g/4oz/1/2 cup caster (superfine) sugar
75g/3oz/1/2 cup crystalized (candied fruit) peel, chopped
50g/2oz/1/3 cup raisins
50g/2oz/1/2 cup chopped blanched almonds
grated rind of 1 lemon
5ml/1 tsp pure vanilla essence (extract)
pared lemon rind and geranium leaves, to decorate
sliced fresh kulich or fruited brioche, to serve

SERVES 8

VARIATION
A mixture of ricotta and mascarpone can be used instead of the curd cheese, and chopped pistachio nuts instead of the almonds.

1 Put the curd cheese, softened butter, egg yolks and caster sugar in a bowl. Whisk until smooth, then mix in the candied fruits, raisins, almonds, lemon rind and vanilla essence.

2 Unless you have a pashka mould, line a clean, new 18cm/7in flower pot with wet muslin. Pack in the mixture. Cover with a plate and weigh down with heavy cans or weights.

3 Place the flower pot on a deep plate and leave to drain overnight at cool room temperature or for a full day in the refrigerator.

4 Discard the whey, then uncover the flower pot and turn it out on to a pretty serving plate. Decorate with pared lemon rind and geranium leaves. To serve, slice horizontally from the top down or cut into thin wedges. Offer sliced fresh kulich or fruited brioche with the pashka.

CARROT CAKE WITH CREAM CHEESE ICING

—

*This moist cut-and-come-again cake has a delicious cream cheese icing.
It makes a rather good grown-up birthday cake.*

*90g/3¹/₂oz/scant 1 cup wholemeal
(whole-wheat) flour
150g/5oz/1¹/₄ cups plain
(all-purpose) flour
10ml/2 tsp baking powder
5ml/1 tsp bicarbonate of soda
5ml/1 tsp ground cinnamon
2.5ml/¹/₂ tsp ground allspice
250g/9oz/1¹/₂ cups brown sugar
3 carrots, coarsely grated
125g/4oz/1 cup chopped walnuts
3 large eggs
juice of 1 orange
120ml/4fl oz/¹/₂ cup sunflower oil
pared orange rind shreds, to decorate*

*FOR THE ICING
50g/2oz/¹/₄ cup butter, softened
200g/7oz/scant 1 cup cream cheese,
softened
grated rind of 1 orange
200g/7oz/1³/₄ cups icing
(confectioner's) sugar
5ml/1 tsp pure vanilla essence (extract)*

SERVES 8

1 Preheat the oven to 180°C/350°F/Gas 4.
Lightly grease a 23cm/9in round cake
tin (pan) and line the base with baking
parchment the paper.

2 Sift all the dry ingredients except the
brown sugar into a bowl, then tip in the
bran from the sieve. Add the brown
sugar, carrots and walnuts.

3 Beat the eggs and orange juice in a
bowl. Make a well in the dry mixture
and add the egg mixture and oil. Mix
well. Spoon into the prepared tin and
level the top. Bake for about 1 hour
until risen and springy to the touch.

4 Slide a knife between the cake and the
tin to loosen it, then turn the cake out
on a rack and remove the lining paper.

5 To make the icing, beat the butter,
cream cheese and grated orange rind in
a large bowl. Sift the icing sugar, then
gradually add to the bowl with the
vanilla essence, beating well after each
addition, until the mixture is creamy.

6 Slice the cake horizontally into two
layers using a large serrated knife.
Sandwich the cake together with about
half the icing, then spread the rest of
the icing on the top, swirling it
attractively with a palette knife. Scatter
the shreds of orange rind around the
edge of the iced cake to decorate.

VARIATION
Instead of using shreds of orange rind
to decorate the cake, sprinkle the iced
cake with a little ground cinnamon,
finely chopped walnuts or coffee
sugar crystals.

INDEX